A Call
To
Unity And Action

(A Collection of verses From the Holy Qur'ãn)

with An Introduction
By
Abdul Jabbar

And A Foreword
By

Sir Syed Sultan Ahmad. KT.

Bar.-at-Law, Patna

KITAB BHAVAN
New Delhi -110002

Kitab Bhavan
Exporters & Importers
1784, Kalan Mahal,
Darya Ganj,
New Delhi-2 [India]

Phones : 3274686, 3277392-93
Fax : 91-11-3263383
E-Mail : nasri @ giasdl01.vsnl.net.in
Telex : 31-63106 ALI IN

ISBN 81-7151-240-2

First Published in India : 1938
Reprinted : 1997

Printed & Published in India by:
Nusrat Ali Nasri for Kitab Bhavan
1784, Kalan Mahal,
Darya Ganj, New Delhi-2 (India)

DEDICATION

Dedicated to the sacred memory of the Holy Saint Khawaja Moin-ud-din Chishti Ajmeri (Peace be on his soul), the Pioneer of Islam in India, revered alike by Hindus and Muslims, whose Khadim, the writer has the privilege to be.

CONTENTS

[*N.B.*– Figures on the left hand represent the number of the Chapter in the Qur'ān ; On the right that of the verse of that Chapter,thus (XXII : 67) means 67th verse of 22nd Surah (Chapter)]

Page.

ACKNOWLEDGMENT

THE English translation of the verses of the Quran selected by me is that of Allama Abdullah Yusuf Ali, C.B.E., M.A., LL.M., I.C.S. (retired), Fellow of the Royal Society of Literature (England). When I wrote to him seeking his permission to use his translation he gave it with great pleasure and I am very grateful to him for this courtesy.

My thanks are also due to my nephew Syed Abdul Ahad Moini, M.A. and to Mr. F. K. Khan Durrani, Editor, *Truth*, Lahore, for the help and encouragement they gave to me, without which I would not have been able to accomplish the task.

Finally I am indebted to M. Muhammad Sadib, Proprietor, Ripon Printing Press, Bull Road, Lahore, and to his staff for the interest they have taken for the careful printing of this brochure.

HAFIZ MANZIL, AJMER — ABDUL JABBAR

Dated, 2nd Sept. 1938.

ACKNOWLEDGEMENT

[illegible]

Dated, 2nd [illegible]

FOREWORD

TRANSLATION is, at best, the wrong side of embroidery; but when it comes to the rendering into a different language of a work of great artistic beauty with its subtle rhythmic nuances the difference between the original and the translation becomes more manifest.

To translate the Quran adequately is well nigh impossible. To start with, the sonorous roll and periodic rhythm of Arabic have no parallel in modern languages, and the Quran represents Arabic at its most musical and suggestive. The most pretentious translation has to despair of recapturing the impassioned cadence and subtle undertones of the Quranic style. Why then translate the Book at all? The answer, alas, is simple. The number of people in India and elsewhere with adequate familiarity with Arabic is dwindling daily—the message of the Quran, however, is eternal, and for the whole world. And so, some medium has to be found out to drive home the immortal truth into the consciousness of too mortal men.

There are numerous translations of the Quran, good, bad, and frankly indifferent. Among the translations that have come to my notice the one which is most persistently capturing some of the tonal qualities of the original, and which is most satisfying as translation is the one by Allama A. Yusuf Ali. And I think, Mr. A. Jabbar has shown praiseworthy discrimination in choosing Allama Yusuf Ali's text for his brochure.

Mr. Jabbar has gone in for simplification. In a volume of very convenient size he has made a small selection from the Quran and arranged the verses under different subject headings so that the reader may easily find verses on any particular matter which are scattered all over the Book culled and bunched together under the appropriate title.

It is necessary to remember, however, that the method has its limitation which I feel sure Mr. Jabbar is well aware of. A verse in the Quran stands in close ideological and tonal relationship with the verses that precede it and those that follow. Its ramifications branch out like the roots of a tree, and all its meaning can only be grasped by realising that it is a part of a greater whole. Any such uprooting as represented in this book necessarily entails the loss of significance and suggestiveness. The reader has to understand fully that no such volume can be a substitute for the Quran. It is only a first step towards the understanding and appreciation of the Divine Book.

This note of warning does not at all imply that the Book does not serve a very definite purpose. There is need, to-day, as at no other time, to make the message of the Quran more universally understood.

And I am sure a perusal of the volume will dissipate a great many of the foggy and wrong-headed notions people entertain about the religion of Islam.

There is one aspect of the Book, however, which has especial significance as Mr. Jabbar rightly suggests in his introduction. Islam means peace. It is the religion of goodwill and tolerance of mutual give-and-take, and harmony in social and spiritual life. By a strange irony of fate false idea has taken roots in the minds of many men—that Islam stands for a religious repression, rancour and a narrow and bigoted prejudice. Unluckily the behaviour of a few so-called followers of Islam might give colour to this misconception. To have made a sincere and convincing effort to eradicate this false notion is in itself a praiseworthy performance.

I congratulate the Editor on having done something very useful adequately. The Book will appeal to all readers who sincerely and honestly believe that sympathetic understanding of the most cherished beliefs and ideals of each other is the only permanent means of peace and happiness for mankind.

PATNA : S. SULTAN AHMED

26th Oct., 1938.

[illegible] of the volume [illegible] a [illegible] motion [illegible]

There is one point of [illegible], however, which has [illegible] rightly [illegible] in his introduction [illegible] many [illegible] of [illegible] intolerance of a [illegible] strange [illegible] for [illegible] of many men—that [illegible] religious [illegible] the [illegible] of a few [illegible] follower of Islam, might [illegible] this [illegible]. To [illegible] and [illegible] effort to eradicate this false notion [illegible]

I congratulate the editor on [illegible] done something very useful adequately. The [illegible] appeal to all readers who sincerely and [illegible] believe in [illegible] understanding [illegible] beliefs and ideals of each other [illegible] of which are [illegible] for humankind.

[illegible] S. [illegible]

[illegible]

INTRODUCTION

I HAVE been thinking for a long time of the dissemination and propagation of the teachings of the Holy Quran. Maulana Abul Kalam Azad in the Introduction to his *Tarjaman-ul-Quran* (Urdu Translation of Quran) writes: "For general study and dissemination it is necessary that the translation of the Quran should be published in different forms and in a variety of editions in such large numbers that Musalmans of every strata of Society and every tract of the country should be able to benefit by it, and no Muslim home should be without a copy of it." These lines provided an impetus for the resolve of mine to collect and publish in a small brochure some of those verses of the Quran which contain injunctions and commandments. I am, therefore, publishing this brochure in the hope that it will prompt the readers to study the Holy Quran with care and thought.

I believe the greatest cause of the decline and downfall of the Muslims is their neglect of the Holy Quran. By decrees the knowledge of the Arabic language declined among them, until they ceased to understand the Holy Quran altogether. One can follow the injunctions of a book only when one understands them. If the order of a court comes to you in a language which you do not know, how will you comply with it ?

God enjoins to read the Quran slowly and to understand it (73 : 4 and to meditate on it (47 : 24). This can best be done when you understand the Arabic language; when however you are not conversant with the language then have recourse to the translation. Mr. Marmaduke Pickthall, who was a life-long student of the Quran, in his English translation *The Glorious Koran* (which is incidentally the first translation of the Quran by an Englishman who is also a Muslim), says :—

"The Koran cannot be translated. That is the belief of old fashioned Sheikhs and the view of the present writer. The book is here rendered almost literally and every effort has been made to choose befitting language. But the result is not the Glorious Koran, that inimitable symphony, the very sounds of which move men to tears and ecstasy. It is only an attempt to present the meaning of the Quran—and per-adventure something of the charm in English. It can never take the place of Koran in Arabic, nor it is meant to do so."

The same is the view of the famous Turkish General Mahmud Muhtar Pasha as noted in *Wisdom of the Quran* written by him in French and translated into English by John Naish, Chief Oriental Reader, Oxford. The celebrated soldier and scholar says :—

"The Quran, in its original Arabic dress, has a beauty and charm of its own. Couched in concise and exalted style, its brief pregnant sentences, often rhymed possess an expressive force and explosive energy which it is extremely difficult to convey by literal word for word translation."

My submission therefore is "Read the Arabic Text with a good translation and gradually you will be able to understand the Text."

History bears witness to the amazing triumph of the Muslims so long as they remained faithful to the teachings of the Holy Quran.

In the lifetime of the Prophet in the year 628 A.D. (6th year of Hijri) the Prophet had sent embassies to the Courts of the Emperors of Rome, Persia and China calling upon them to acknowledge the one true God and to serve Him alone. In the same year a mosque was built in Canton (China) at a distance of about 8,000 miles from Mecca, which survives to this day. It is one of the oldest mosques in the world.

One historian has estimated that within twelve years of the death of the Holy Prophet (11 A.H.= 632 A.D.), *i.e.*, by the close of the reign of Omar the Great (23 A.H.=644 A.D.) the Muslims had conquered thirty-six thousand towns and forts. The rule of Caliph Omar extended over twenty-two million square miles. Within a hundred years of the Prophet's *Hijrat* from Mecca to Medina the Muslims had spread over three continents, stretching in the east to the banks of the Indus and in the west to the south of France, while the whole of North Africa owned their sway. In fact, within one hundred years they had subjugated almost the whole of the then civilized world, except India and the Roman Empire.

It was the spirit born, in them, of a true understanding of the Quran which made the Muslims cheerfully suffer the brutal persecutions and merciless tortures and oppressions to which they were subjected in the early days of Islam, a full narrative of which may be seen in the *Seerat-un-Nabi* of the late Maulana Shibli. The chief fact to be noted in this connection is that these barbarous persecutions failed to induce even one Muslim to objure his faith. A Christian historian says truly: " It would be well for Christians to remember that Muhammad inspired his followers with such an unshakable faith as it would be vain to look for among the first disciples of Jesus Christ. When Jesus was taken to the Cross all his disciples fled and left their master to his gruesome fate. On the other hand the followers of Muhammad rallied round their persecuted prophet, sacrificed their lives in his protection and finally made him triumph over his enemies" (*Apology for Mohammed* by Godfrey Higgins).

The whole basis of the law of Islam is spiritual purification and moral training, equity and good conscience. Islam teaches to make the best of all things, to avoid the foolish, to seek refuge in God, to touch not the goods of an orphan, to covet not another's goods, to abstain from adultery, and to keep your eyes away from lustful objects, to avoid vanity, to give alms, to offer prayers, to show kindliness and respect to one's parents, to avoid iniquity, to be neither unjust nor violent, to seek the pardon of God and to turn to Him for He is merciful and loving, to call upon the Lord in loneliness and in secret. Islam as preached in the Quran is the religion that helps man to live in peace with himself, and in peace with his fellows and the rest of creation.

A few special characteristics of the religion, the Quran teaches, may be recounted here:—

Firstly, Islam may boast of a catholicity peculiar to itself namely that, in order to be a good Muslim, it is not necessary to reject the truth or veracity of other religions revealed to the world before the Quran. The Quran does not set out new ideas, not already known to mankind.

Secondly, Islam is a religion easy of comprehension. A Muslim is required to believe in one God, in the truth as revealed in the Quran and the

Scriptures that have preceded it. It does not lay down an elaborate ritual beyond the grasp of the man in the street.

Thirdly parochialism or any notion of the favoured nation has no place in the teachings of Islam. Parochialism is the creation of the brain of Mullas and self-styled Molvies. There is no honour by birth, or disgrace by colour, race or language. There is but one criterion of greatness open to all alike. " Surely the noblest amongst you in the eyes of God is one who is most mindful of his duty" (Quran).

Fourthly, Islam establishes a brotherhood among Muslims—" No one among you is a believer in God unless he loves his brother as he loves himself."

Fifthly, Islam is a religion of peace and toleration. The dominant feature of Islam as its name implies, is the making of peace.

Sixthly, Islam is not merely the elaboration of theory—it is a code of practical ethics and a guide to daily life. To be a good Muslim, the practical is as essential as the theoretical, mere belief being insufficient.

Seventhly, Islam eradicates various injustices of a social nature, and attempts to establish the most equitable social order in the world.

Eighthly, Islam is a religion which takes account of human nature.

Ninthly, Islam lays much stress on the acquisition and cultivation of knowledge by men and women. The Prophet says:—" He who goes abroad in the search of knowledge is in the path of God till he returns." " It is incumbent on every male or female to acquire knowledge." "The ink of scholar is more holy than the blood of the martyr." And again, "Acquire knowledge, it will enable you to distinguish right and wrong, it will light the way to heaven; it will be your friend in the desert, your society in solitude, your companion in loneliness, your guide to happiness, the sustainer of your misery, the ornament among your friends, and the armour against your enemies" (*Hadis*, *i.e.*, sayings of the Prophet).

Mohammad, in distinction to other Prophets before him, passed through all the phases of life from orphan to king, from idealist to the man of the world. His amazing career has embraced the position of a son, a father, a husband, a neighbour, a shepherd, a tradesman, a preacher, a persecuted fugitive, a friend, a warrior, a general, a judge, an administrator, a law-giver, a statesman and then an Emperor. It is because of his wonderful spiritual power that though unlettered, yet, in his life he filled all these roles.

In Quran God says to the Holy Prophet, "We sent thee not, but as a mercy for all creatures" (XXI: 107). Hear what the messenger of God himself points out, says he: "Respect the ways of Allah, and be affectionate to the family of Allah; All creatures of God are His family and he is the most beloved of God who loveth best His creatures" (Hadis).

Such, then, is the Islam for which Mr. C. F. Andrews, observes in a recent contribution, "The Function of Islam:"

"One of the greatest blessings which Islam has brought to the East and the West alike has been the emphasis which at a critical period in human history is placed upon the Divine Unity. For during those Dark Ages, both in East and West, from 600 to 1000 A.D. this doctrine was in danger of being overlaid and obscured in Hinduism and in Christianity itself, owing to the immense accretions of subsidiary worships of countless demi-gods and heroes. Islam has been both, to Europe and to India in their darkest hour of aberration from the sovereign truth of God's Unity, an invaluable corrective and deterrent. Indeed, without the final emphasis on this truth, which Islam gave from its central position, facing India and facing Europe, it is doubtful whether this idea of God as one could have obtained that established place in human thought which is uncontested in the intellectual world to-day." (*The Genuine Islam*, Singapore, Vol. I ; No 8, 1936.)

Again this is the Islam for which Bernard Shaw says : "I have always held the religion of Muhammad in high estimation because of its wonderful vitality. It is the only religion which appears to me to possess that assimilating capability to the changing phase of existence which can make itself appeal to every age. I have studied him—the wonderful man, and in my opinion, far from being an Anti-Christ, he must be called the Saviour of Humanity. I believe that if a man like him were to assume the dictatorship of the modern world, he would succeed in solving its problems in a way that would bring it the much-needed peace and happiness, I have prophesied about the faith of Muhammad that it would be acceptable to the Europe of tomorrow, as it is beginning to be acceptable to the Europe of to-day." (*The Genuine Islam*, Singapore, Vol. I; No. 1, 1936).

Jean Lheureux, says at Page 35 of *Etude sur Islamisme*, "Islam had the power of peacefully conquering the souls by the simplicity of its theology, the clearness of its dogma and principles, and the definite number of the practices which it demands. In contrast to Christianity which has been undergoing continual transformation since its origin, Islam has remained identical with itself."

A whole volume could be filled with such quotations but the space does not allow me to quote any more on this subject.

The early triumphs of Islam owed themselves in the main to the self-sacrifice and unity of the Muslims and their obedience to their Chief. When these virtues declined, their power also began to wane. Unity is essential to national well-being, and as the Holy Quran states expressly in Sura IX : 107-108, it is forbidden even to build a mosque if that mosque causes disunity among Muslims. Mirza Abdul Karim Zanjani one of the leading Mujtahids of Najaf, has written a disquisition on the decline of the Musalmans, in which he has emphasised the necessity of Shia-Sunni unity. The discourse appeared in the *Islamic Review* for April 1936, from which Dr. Zaki Ali has quoted passages in *Islam in the World*. Mr. Zanjani writes:—

" Firstly let me speak to the Shiahs. Brethren, you have exceeded the limits of propriety, for you have far exceeded the example set by your Imam Hazrat Ali (peace of Allah be upon him). Hazrat Ali was a claimant to the Khilafat, but we have his most definite and unequivocal pronouncement on the supreme need of keeping the unity of Islam intact. All the differences should be for, and not against, Islam. In *Nehajul Balaghat*, the sovereign lord of Souls, Hazrat Imam Ali says, " I co-operated with sincere faith and perfect unity of heart with Abu Bakr, Omar and Usman, the three early Caliphs, in the transaction of high matters of state and religion; so much so, that when they sat, I sat, when they stood up, I stood up, and when they marched forward, I marched forward. Whenever they sought my help, I offered my services. I never grudged to give them my counsel; Nay, I often worked as their Vicegerent in the capital of Medina in their absence.

"This is the ideal of unity and co-operation which every true lover and follower of Hazrat Imam should treasure in his heart and mind, and practise in his social life.

"To my Sunni brethren-in-faith, I would like to say, You boast of building the organizations and empires of Islam. How, then, is it possible that you are now engaged in controversies which should be far from the minds of broad-visioned and high-souled statesmen? As elder brothers, yours is the major responsibility for maintaining and perfecting the unity of Islam.

"Schism and religious factionism has been the curse of Muslims. It is nothing short of waging war with Allah and the Prophet of Allah. It is the fatal disease of your body-politic. You must either tear it out root and branch, or be prepared to become the victims of the anti-Islamic onslaughts coming from the West and from Russia."

Allama Inayat Ullah Khan Mashriqi, leader of the Khaksar Movement says, "I am convinced that the Holy Quran, in the rationality, wisdom and comprehensiveness of its teaching, is matchless, and no development of human knowledge can surpass it."

Revealed scriptures generally deal with one or other aspect of religion, but this matchless scripture presents the whole of it. There is no phase or aspect of social life, culture and Civilization, for the development and maintenance of which the Holy Quran does not contain full and frequent teachings. It contains unerring guidance for social peace and domestic happiness in times of peace and war. It is a complete guidance, it is a mine of truth and wisdom, clear, perspicuous, easy to comprehend, free of inconsistencies, altogether beyond the power of man to produce the like of it. It is a mercy, a light and healing for those who think and ponder over it. It is no small argument for its divine origin that though the Quran was revealed Sura by Sura and section by section in the course of twenty-three years in most varied circumstances and situations, there is the most perfect agreement between its various parts in language as well as in teachings. It is for us, therefore, to ponder over it, find its true meaning and act upon it.

Islam came to remove all differences from among the peoples of the world and unite them into one brotherhood on a basis of complete equality between man and man.

The beauty of the Quran consists in its matchless teachings. The Quran lays down that Faith is essential for gaining life everlasting, and God's promise of assistance in the here, and salvation in the hereafter is for those whose faith is sound, and who with sound faith act righteously. That community alone deserves to be called righteous whose members possess both these qualifications, and Islam which is the law of nature assures integrity and safety only to such a community. Where the Quran demands belief, it also commands that the believers should act virtuously.

The Quran says again and again in Sura Baqar that the divine religion is a religion of practical righteousness, and man is rewarded with only what he strives for. The fact that one's race has given birth to many prophets and saints, or that one is descendant from saintly ancestors or is connected with some ancient race, has no value whatever for one's salvation or spiritual purity.

The West is acting upon some of the principles of the Quran and is reaping the harvest of God's blessings. The Muslims are not acting upon any principle and are therefore declining rapidly. They have lost all conception of Divine unity and the consequence is that there is no unity among them. They do not obey. The spirit of sacrifice, and steadfastness, high morals, the desire for betterment and the zeal of faith have all disappeared from among them, and the glorious rose garden of Islam has become a house of despondency, defection and mourning, because the Muslims have forgotten the purposes of the Quran and have strayed far and away from the true signification of faith and purc living.

Maulana Abul Kalam Azad, in his commentary on Sura Fatiha, says, "At the time the Holy Quran was revealed, four religious conceptions ruled the human mind, *viz.*, Indian, Magian, Jewish and Christian. The religious philosophy of the Upanishads holds a prominent place in the Indian conception of religion. The Upanishads are the most ancient source of the doctrine of pantheism. Whatever may be the age of the Gita, its teachings are but an echo of the Upanishads. Pantheism presents a very strange view of the Deity. While on the one hand it declares everything to be "God" because it denies the existence of everything apart from God who alone truly exists, on the other hand, it gives no clear and well-defined conception of God. In any case, this conception of God was so abstract and metaphysical in nature that in no time or country did it succeed in becoming an article of faith with the commonalty. Even in India it never attained any higher status than that of being one school of philosophy among many. The best interpretation that has been put upon this state of affairs is that the worship of idols was prescribed for the common people, while pantheism became the faith of philosophic minds".

The doctrine of Divine Unity is to be found also in the Sanatan Dharm. Several stories are current among the Sanatanists, which prove that the doctrine of divine unity exists among them. The well-known Hindu festival of *Holi* is a memorial of Prahlad's devotion to one God. The story is to be found in Bhagwat Puran and may be stated briefly as follows: Prahlad's father Harnakush claimed to be God and commanded that people should worship him and no other God. When Prahlad repeated the name of God, he was put to tortures, but suffered not in the least. As he persisted in worshipping God, he was cast into fire, but came out safe and unhurt. The moral of the story is obvious ; but if the Hindus refuse to understand it, it is no fault of the Muslims if they also fail to understand the real significance of the festival of Holi. And it is on this occasion of Holi that communal fracases take place. It certainly is no fault of religion.

Similarly, take Muharram which Musalmans celebrate as a festival, and on which, instead of weeping and wailing, there take place Hindu-Muslim riots, Shias and Sunnis fight, and every year the Government has to spend large sums of money on the prevention of such disorders. Such disorders are a necessary consequence of the manner in which Muharram is celebrated in India. Prior to the horrible tragedy of Karbela, Arabs used to celebrate an Id-festival in the first ten days of Muharram. After the martyrdom of the exalted Imam the same days of rejoicing were turned into days of sorrow and pain. It was quite natural that it should be so because of the unforgettable sufferings of the Prophet's grandson and his family on the burning sand of Karbela. But the Musalmans of to-day, instead of a sincere remembrance of the great Imam and taking him as a model to follow, spend the day generally in frivolity. Let the Musalmans ponder over the great sacrifice of Imam Husain (on whom be peace and the blessings of Allah) and the circumstances that led to it, and compare it with the manner in which they celebrate his memory to-day.

Let everybody remember that neither the Muslims can wipe out the Hindus by these communal riots nor can the Hindus exterminate the Muslims. Both have to live side by side in India, and both must equally suffer by their mutual dispute.

With a view to bring about the desired re-approachment I have purposely given the translation of the Quranic verses in English in order that non-Muslim fellow country-men of mine should also be able to read them, and I wish to warn them hereby against incorrect translations and false propaganda from whatever quarter the same might proceed. If Mahmud the Ghaznavide plundered Hindu temples, it was his personal act and is not approved by Islam. I may suggest to the reader here to read the life of Sultan Mahmud by Prof. Habib of the Muslim University, Aligarh, who has pointed out all those actions of the Sultan, which were against the teachings of Islam. Let the Hindus consider the great harm the inter-communal disputes do to the country at large and not to pick up quarrels in the name of religion. Do not look to the misdeeds of a few through the glasses prepared for you by interested historians with the object of sowing the seeds of discord. Root out the plants that have grown out of those seeds. It will be good for all. If some have misbehaved, there are many who have done good to you and there is a lot of literature in support of this contention.

Maulana Abul Kalam Azad writes in his commentary on Sura Fatiha : " According to the Quran, differences of religion are of two kinds. One kind is the difference which the followers of various religions have created by deviating from the true teachings of religion. Differences of this type are not differences of religions. They are rather the consequence of the follower's straying from religion. The other kind is the differences between the teachings and the practices prescribed by various religions. For instance, one religion prescribes one form of worship, while another religion prescribes another form. This is a difference of external forms and not of inner reality, and it was quite natural that this difference should come into existence. According to the Quran the teachings of religion consist of two different things. One is the inner reality, the other is their external form. The first is fundamental; the other is secondary. The first it calls religion. The other it terms فرع and نسك. Another word used for the same is شرع منهاج and منهاج means "path", and نسك means the mode of worship. According to the Quran the differences of religion, so far as they are real, are differences not of religion, but of the secondary appurtenances, not of inner reality but of outer manifestations, not of spirit but of form; and these differences are of natural growth.

"The purpose of religion is the betterment and spiritual purification of the human society, but the conditions of the human society have not been the same in every age and country, nor can they remain always alike. The cultural and mental capacity of one age differs from that of another, and the manner of life differs from country to country. Therefore the advent of a religion in one particular age among a people of a certain capacity and temperament necessitated the formulation of laws suited to them, and whatever laws and forms were adopted in a certain age and country were best suited to that age and country. Therefore every form is good in its own place, and this difference has no greater importance than the cultural and natural differences of the various groups of humanity. The Holy Quran says: To every people have We appointed rites and ceremonies*

* Rites and ceremonies may appear to be an unimportant matter compared with "weightier matters of the Law" and with the higher needs of man's spiritual nature. But they are

which they must follow : let them not then dispute with thee on the matter, but do thou invite (them) to thy Lord : for thou art assuredly on the Right way (XXII : 67). When the change of the Qibla took place and the Holy Prophet faced towards the Kaaba in prayer instead of towards Bethlehem, the Jews and Christians felt much hurt at it, because in their view religion depended entirely upon these external formalities which they looked upon as the sole criterion of right and wrong. But we find that the Quran looks at the question from quite a different point of view and says that we should attach no importance to it at all ; for these external forms cannot be the criterion of truth and falsehood, nor do they have any place in the essentials of religion. Every religion adopted a mode of worship in keeping with its own peculiar requirements and circumstances. The purpose of all is the same, *viz.*, the worship of God and righteous living. Let him, therefore, who is in search of truth keep his eye on the real and ultimate purpose. Now a question arises : If the aim and object of all religions is the same and all are based on truth, where was the necessity for the revelation of the Quran ? The Holy Book gives the answer and says that though all revealed religions are true, the followers of those religions had gone astray from truth ; it was therefore necessary to bring them all back to the truth. Three things are prominent among those fundamental principles on which the Quran lays great stress in this

necessary for social and religious organization, and their effect on the individual himself is not to be despised. In any case, as they are visible external symbols, they give rise to the most heated controversy. Such controversies are to be deprecated. That does not mean that our rites and ceremonies are to be made light of. Those in Islam rest on the highest social and religious needs of man, and if we are convinced that we are on the Right Way, we should invite all to join us, without entering into controversies about such matters.

connection, *viz.* : (1) The salvation and eternal happiness of man depends upon faith and deeds and not upon belonging to any race or group. (2) For mankind there is only one religion, and its teachings have been dispensed to all alike. The mutually opposed groups and sects which the followers of religions have formed by ignoring the unity of divine truth are therefore a manifest error. (3) The real religion is the unity of God, that is, the worship of the Creator and Lord of the world direct. All founders of religions have taught the same. All beliefs and practices opposed to this basic principle are an error and divergence from true religion. The Holy Quran teaches in express and quite unequivocal words that Jews and Christians, Magians and Brahmans, in short the followers of all religions are entitled to their rewards here and hereafter in proportion to the excellence of their deeds. It declares them all to be creation of the same one God and thereby seeks to establish unity and equality among them ".

Blasphemy in the Spiritual Kingdom is like treason in the political kingdom and God forgiveth not the sin of joining other gods with Him. But He forgiveth whom He pleaseth other sins than this. (IV : 48 and 116).

All religions came from the same source. God Almighty says in the Holy Quran that He sent His apostles to every race and country, some of whom are mentioned in the Quran, while many others are not so mentioned.

I intended to make the introduction brief. It has become long, while I feel much still remains untold. The shortcomings and ailments of the Muslim community are many. Their social corruption, national poverty, vocational backwardness, absence of organization, mutual differences and *moral weakness*, etc., are evils crying for remedies. On the other hand, the political conditions of India are changing rapidly. If the Musalmans do not take swift measures to remedy these conditions, their future appears to be hopeless.

It is my prayer that the followers of various religions in India should live in amity and goodwill with one another, and that the same atmosphere of tolerance, mutual sympathy, regard and good fellowship should prevail in our country as it does in Egypt and other countries. I have lived in the hope that the Hindu-Muslim Unity of 1920-21 might be re-established among us.

I fear the Muslims of India have sunk so deep that the time for speeches and writing is past. The situation calls for immediate action. I do not claim to be a scholar or an author. Only my heart has felt the sting of the present sorrowful conditions and I have resolved to make this appeal to my co-religionists and fellow countrymen. May God Almighty accept this humble service and move my fellow countrymen to listen to this appeal and act upon it.

There are several translations of the Quran in the English language by non-Muslims, anti-Muslims and Muslims. I went through most of them. Some of them are written with the sole object of causing mischief. I selected Allama Yusuf Ali's translation, as the best and I have used his translation. Innumerable appreciative reviews and encomiums have, from time to time, appeared in the press for Allama's translation and it is needless for me to say more about it, and I leave it to the kind readers to judge.

I have followed, in punctuation and numbering of verses, the Text prepared by Anjuman Himayatul Islam, Lahore, which I consider the most carefully prepared Text ever printed in India.

HAFIZ MANZIL AJMER ABDUL JABBAR.

Dated, 2nd Sept. 1938.

(In the name of God, most Gracious, most Merciful.)

VERSES FROM THE HOLY QURAN

I.—ALLAH ENJOINS TO—

AVOID VAIN TALKS, ETC.

XXIII : 1 to 9

1. The Believers must
(Eventually) win through,—[1]
2. Those who humble themselves[2]
In their Prayers ;
3. Who avoid vain talk ;
4. Who are active in deeds
Of charity ;
5. Who abstain from sex,[3]
6. Except with those joined
to them in the marriage bond,

1. *Aflaha* : win through, prosper, succeed, achieve their aims or obtain salvation from sorrow and all evil. This verse connects on with verses 10 and 11 below. The success or victory may come in this world, but is certain and lasting in the world to come.

2. Humility in prayer as regards (1) their estimate of their own worth in God's presence, (2) as regards their estimate of their own powers or strength unless they are helped by God, and (3) as regards the petitions they offer to God.

3. The Muslim must guard himself against every kind of sex abuse or sex pervertion. The new psychology associated with the name of Freud traces many of our hidden motives to sex, and it is common knowledge that our refinement or degradation may be measured by the hidden workings of our sex instincts. But even the natural and lawful exercise of sex is restricted to the marriage bond, under which the rights of both parties are duly regulated and maintained.

Or (the captives) whom
Their right hands possess,—[4]
For (in their case) they are
Free from blame,
7. But those whose desires exceed
Those limits are transgressors;—
8. Those who faithfully observe
Their trusts and their covenants;[5]
9. And who (strictly) guard[6]
Their Prayers;—

SPEND IN CHARITY

III : 180

And let not those
Who covetously withhold

4. This is further explained and amplified in iv : 25. It will be seen there that the status of a captive when raised to freedom by marriage is the same as that of a free woman as regards her rights, but more lenient as regards the punishment to be inflicted if she falls from virtue.

5. Trusts may be express or implied. Express trusts are those where property is entrusted or duties are assigned by some one to some other whom he trusts, to carry out either immediately or in specified contingencies, such as death. Implied trusts arise out of power, or position, or opportunity; *e.g.*, a king holds his kingdom on trust from God for his subjects; the Afghan Official phrase for their kingdom used to be *Daulat-e-Khudadad* ('God-given Kingdom'). Covenants create obligations, and express and implied trusts and covenants taken together cover the whole field of obligations.

6. In verse 2 we are directed to the spirit of humility and earnestness in our prayers. Here we are told how necessary the habit of regular prayer is to our spiritual well-being and development, as it brings us closer to God, and thus sums up the light of the seven jewels of our Faith, *viz.* : (1) humility, (2) avoidance of vanity, (3) charity, (4) sex purity, (5) fidelity to

Of the gifts which God
Hath given them of His Grace[7]
Think that it is good for them:
Soon shall the things
Which they covetously withheld
Be tied to their necks
Like a twisted collar,[8]
On the Day of Judgment.
To God belongs the heritage[9]
Of the heavens and the earth;
And God is well-acquainted
With all that ye do.

tursts, and (6) to covenants, and (7) an earnest desire to get closer to God.

7. The gifts are of all kinds: material gifts, such as wealth, property, strength of limbs, etc., or intangible gifts such as influence, birth in a given set, intellect, skill, insight, etc., or spiritual gifts of the highest kind. The spending of all these things (apart from what is necessary for ourselves) for those who need them, is charity, and purifies our own character. The withholding of them (apart from our needs) is similarly greed and selfishness, and is strongly condemned.

8. By an apt metaphor the miser is told that his wealth or the other gifts which he hoarded will cling round his neck and do him no good. He will wish he could get rid of them, but he will not be able to do so. According to the Bibilical phrase in another connection they will hang like a millstone round his neck (Matt. xviii : 6). The metaphor here is fuller. He hugged his wealth of his gifts about him. They will become like a heavy collar, the badge of slavery, round his neck. They will be tied tight and twisted, and they will give him pain and anguish instead of pleasure.

9. Another metaphor is now introduced. Material wealth or property is only called ours during our short life here: it then descends to heirs and heirs until it goes to the ultimate heir, the State. So all gifts are ours, in trust only; they ultimately revert to God, to Whom belongs all that is in the heavens or on earth.

II : 215

They ask thee
What they should spend
(In Charity). Say : " Whatever
Ye spend that is good,[10]
Is for parents and kindred
And orphans
And those in want
And for wayfarers.

II : 261

The parable of those,
Who spend their substance
In the way of God is that
Of a grain of corn : it groweth
Seven ears, and each ear
Hath a hundred grains.
God giveth manifold increase
To whom He pleaseth :
For God careth for all,
And He knoweth all things.

10. Three questions arise in charity: (1) What shall we give? (2) to whom shall we give? and (3) how shall we give? The answer is here. Give anything that is good, useful, helpful, valuable. It may be property or money; it may be a helping hand; it may be advice; it may be a kind word; " whatever ye do that is good " is charity. On the other hand, if you throw away what is useless, there is no charity in it. Or if you give something with a harmful intent, *e.g.*, a sword to a madman, or a drug or sweets or even money to some one whom you want to entrap or corrupt, it is no charity but a gift of damnation. To whom should you give? It may be tempting to earn the world's praise by a gift that will be talked about, but are you meeting the needs of those who have the first claim on you? If you are not, you are like a person who defrauds creditors: it is no charity. Every gift is judged by its unselfish character: the degree of

XXX : 38

So give what is due
To kindred, the needy,
And the wayfarer.
That is best for those
Who seek the Countenance
Of God, and it is they
Who will prosper.

XVII : 29

Make not thy hand tied [11]
(Like a niggard's) to thy neck,
Nor stretch it forth
To its utmost reach,
So that thou become
Blameworthy and destitute.

II : 267

O ye who believe!
Give of the good things
Which ye have (honourably) earned,[12]
And of the fruits of the earth

need or claim is a factor which you should consider; if you disregard it, there is something selfish behind it. How should it be given? As in the sight of God; this shuts out all pretence, show, and insincerity.

11. We are not to be so lavish as to make ourselves destitute and incur the just censure of wise men, nor is it becoming to keep back our resources from the just needs of those who have a right to our help. Even strangers have such a right. But we must keep a just measure between our capacity and other people's needs.

12. According to the English proverb "Charity covers a multitude of sins." Such a sentiment is strongly disapproved

Which We have produced
For you, and do not even aim [13]
At getting anything
Which is bad, in order that
Out of it ye may give away
Something, when ye yourselves
Would not receive it
Except with closed eyes.[14]

in Islam. Charity has value only if (1) something good and valuable is given, (2) which has been honourably earned or acquired by the giver, or (3) which is produced in nature and can be referred to as a bounty of God. (1) may include such things as are of use and value to others, though they may be of less use to us or superfluous to us on account of our having acquired something more suitable for our station in life; for example, discarded clothes, or an old horse or a used motor car; but if the horse is vicious, or the car engine so far gone that it is dangerous to use, then the gift is worse than useless; it is positively harmful, and the giver is a wrong-doer. (2) applies to fraudulent company promoters, who earn great credit by giving away in charity some of their ill-gotten gains, or to robbers (even if they call themselves by high sounding names) who "rob Peter to pay Paul." Islam will have nothing to do with tainted property. Its economic code requires that every gain should be honest and honourable. Even "charity" would not cover or destroy the taint. (3) lays down a test in cases of a doubtful gain. Can we refer to it as a gift of God? Obviously the produce of honest labour or agriculture can be so referred to. In modern commerce and speculation there is much of quite the contrary character, and charity will not cover the taint. Some kinds of art, skill, or talent are God-given: it is the highest kind of charity to teach them or share their product. Others are the contrary, they are bad or tainted. In the same way some professions or services may be tainted, if these tend to moral harm.

13. The preceding note tries to indicate some of the things which are bad or tainted. We should not even think of acquiring them for ourselves, soothing our conscience by the salve that we shall practise charity out of them.

14. *Closed eyes* imply disgust or connivance because of some feature which we would not openly acknowledge.

And know that God
Is Free of all wants,
And Worthy of all praise.[15]

II : 273

(Charity is) for those
In need, who, in God's cause [16]
Are restricted (from travel)
And cannot move about
In the land, seeking
For trade or work :
The ignorant man thinks,
Because of their modesty,
That they are free from want.
Thou shalt know them
By their (unfailing) mark :
They beg not importunately
From all and sundry.
And whatever of good
Ye give, be assured
God knoweth it well.

15. To dedicate tainted things to God is a dishonour to God, Who is independent of all wants, and Who is worthy of all honour and praise.

16. Indiscriminate acts of so-called charity are condemned as they may do more harm than good. The real benificiaries of charity are here indicated. They must be in want. And the want must be due to some honourable cause. For example, they may be doing some unpaid service, such as teaching, or acquiring knowledge or skill, or be in exile for their faith, or in other ways be prevented from seeking employment or doing strenuous work. "God's cause" must not be narrowly interpreted. All sincere and real service to humanity comes within the definition, as well as actual devotion to religion or to the righteous Imam. Such men do not beg from door to door. It is the duty of those who are well-to-do, or of the Public Purse, to find them out.

DO YOUR DUTY

XXXI : 33

O mankind ! do your duty
To your Lord and fear
(The coming of) a Day
When no father can avail
Aught for his son, nor
a son avail aught
For his father.[17]
Verily, the promise of God
Is true : let not then
This present life deceive you,
Nor let the Chief Deceiver[18]
Deceive you about God.

DO GOOD

IV : 36

Serve God, and join not[19]
Equals with Him ;

17. On the Day of Reckoning no one can help another. The most loving father cannot help his son or be a substitute for him, and *vice versa*. Each will have his own personal responsibilities.

18. The Chief Deceiver is the Power of Evil. It may make us forget that Time is fleeting and delude us by suggesting that the Reckoning may not come, whereas it is certain to come, because God's promise is true. We must not play with Time nor be deceived by appearances. The Day may come to-day or tomorrow, or when we least expect it.

19. The essence of Islam is to serve God and do good to your fellow creatures. This is wider and more comprehensive than "Love God and love your neighbour." For it includes duties to animals as our fellow-creatures, and emphasises practical service rather than sentiment.

And do good—
To parents, kinsfolk,
Orphans, those in need
Neighbours who are near,[20]
Neighbours who are strangers,
The Companion by your side,[21]
The way-farer (ye meet),
And what your right hands possess :—[22]
For God loveth not
The arrogant, the vainglorious ;[23]

ESCHEW ALL SIN

VI : 120

Eschew all sin,
Open or secret :

20. *Neighbours who are near* : that is, in local situation as well as intimate relationships, just as *neighbours who are strangers* includes those whom we do not know or who live away from us or in a different sphere altogether.

21. The *Companion by your side* may be your intimate friends and associates, just as the *way-farer you meet* may be a casual acquaintance on your travels. This last is much wider than the "stranger within your gate."

22. *What your right hands possess* : anything that has no civil rights. It includes captives or slaves (where they exist in any form whatever), people in your power, or dumb animals with whom you have to deal. They are all God's creatures and deserve our sympathy and our practical service. *Cf.* Coleridge's "Rime of the Ancient Mariner": "He prayeth best who loveth best All things both great and small, For the dear God Who loveth us, He made and loveth all."

23. Real deeds of service and kindness proceed, not from showing off or from a superior sort of condescension (*Cf.* "White Man's Burden"), but from a frank recognition of our own humility and the real claims, before God, of all our fellow-creatures. For in our mutual needs we are equal before God,

Those who earn sin
Will get due recompense
For their " earnings."

FORGIVE

XLII : 40 to 43

40. The recompense for an injury
Is an injury equal thereto [24]
(In degree) : but if a person
Forgives and makes reconciliation,

or perhaps the best of us (as the world sees us) may be worse than the worst of us (from the same point of view).

24. When you stand up for rights, either on private or public grounds, it may be through processes of law, or by way of private defence in so far as the law permits private action. But in all cases you must not seek a compensation greater than the injury suffered. The most you can do is to demand equal redress, *i.e*, a harm equivalent to the harm done to you. Even this may serve to curb your unregenerate soul, or a community bent on revenge. But the ideal mode is not to slake your thirst for vengeance but to follow better ways leading to the reform of the offender or his reconciliation. You can take steps to prevent repetition, by physical or moral means; the best moral means would be to turn hatred into friendship by forgiveness and love. In that case the compensation or reward (if we must use such terms) is infinitely greater, for it wins the good pleasure of God.

But this active righting of wrongs, whether by physical or by moral or spiritual means, which are commended as better, is an antithesis to the monkish doctrine, when you are smitten on one cheek, to turn the other also. This would not suppress, but encourage wrong-doing. It is practised by none but poltroons, and is preached only by hypocrites, or men who want to make slaves of others by depriving them of the power of self-defence. It occurs in two of the four canonical Gospels (Matt. v. 39 and Luke vi. 29), but we need not therefore assume that it was preached by Jesus.

His reward is due [25]
From God : for (God)
Loveth not those who
Do wrong.[26]

41. But indeed if any do help
And defend themselves
After a wrong (done)
To them, against such [27]
There is no cause
Of blame.

42. The blame is only [28]
Against those who oppress
Men with wrong-doing
And insolently transgress
Beyond bounds through the land,
Defying right and justice :
For such there will be
A Penalty grievous.
But indeed if any

25. To love God is the highest motive of our conduct, for it leads to the love of God's creatures; to win the approbation and love of God, is the highest reward, for transcending any compensation or satisfaction we can obtain in this life.

26. God does not love those who do wrong. If, therefore, we tolerate wrong, or encourage wrong by allowing it to run rampant when we can prevent it, we fail in our duty to God.

27. Such people are not to be blamed, though they are following the lower law. The blame is on those who arrogantly ride rough-shod over the land, oppressing people with grievous wrong. See next verse.

28. The fact that men seek the lower rather than the higher Law is itself a result of arrogant wrong-doing, or which the type was the Pharaoh who claimed to be "your Lord Most High" and oppressed the Israelites, and kept his own people under slavery and subjection, and the false glamour of magic and deception.

43. Show patience and forgive,[29]
That would truly be
An exercise of courageous will
And resolution in the conduct
Of affairs.

III : 133 to 135

133. Be quick in the race
For forgiveness from your Lord,
And for a Garden whose width
Is that (of the whole)
Of the heavens
And of the earth,[30]
Prepared for the righteous,—

29. It is harder to be patient and forgive, and yet to get wrongs righted, as was done by the Holy Prophet, than to bluster about and "punish the guilty" or "teach them lessons". It may look like futility or lack of purpose, but in reality it is the highest and noblest form of courage and resolution. And it may carry out the purpose of reform and the suppression of evil even better than stern punishment. The gentleness of innocence often "pursuades where stronger measures fail." But of course circumstances alter cases, and there is some allowance also to be made for the personal equation of the men you have to deal with: in some cases severity may be called for, but it should be from a strict judicial motive, and not merely from personal anger or spite or any lower motive in disguise.

30. The Fire is, as always contrasted with the Garden in a spiritual sense,—in other words, Hell contrasted with Heaven. Lest we should think that heaven is a sort of enclosed material Garden somewhere in the skies, we are told that its width alone is that of the whole of the heavens and earth,—all the creation we can imagine. In other words our spiritual felicity covers not merely this or that part of our being, but all life and all existence. Who can measure its width, or length, or depth ?

134. Those who spend (freely),[31]
Whether in prosperity,
Or in adversity;
Who restrain anger,
And pardon (all) men;—
For God loves those
Who do good;—
135. And those who,[32]
Having done something
To be ashamed of,
Or wronged their own souls,[33]
Earnestly bring God to mind,
And ask for forgiveness
For their sins,—
And who can forgive

31. Another definition of the righteous (*vv.* 134-35). So far from grasping material wealth, they give freely, of themselves and their substance, not only when they are well-off and it is easy for them to do so, but also when they are in difficulties, for other people may be in difficulties at the same time. They do not get ruffled in adversity, or get angry when other people behave badly, or their own good plans fail. On the contrary they redouble their efforts. For the charity—or good deed—is all the more necessary in adversity. And they do not throw the blame on others. Even where such blame is due and correction is necessary, their own mind is free from a sense of grievance, for they forgive and cover other men's faults. This as far as other people are concerned. But we may be ourselves at fault, and perhaps we brought some calamity on ourselves. The righteous man is not necessarily perfect. In such circumstances his behaviour is described in the next verse.

32. The righteous man, when he finds he has fallen into sin or error, does not whine or despair, but asks for God's forgiveness, and his faith gives him hope. If he is sincere, that means that he abandons his wrong conduct and makes amends.

33. Sin is a sort of oppression of ourselves by ourselves. This follows from the doctrine of personal responsibility, as opposed to that of blind fate or of an angry God or gods lying in wait for revenge or injury on mankind.

Sins except God?—
And are never obstinate
In persisting knowingly
In (the wrong) they have done.

GREET (STILL MORE COURTEOUSLY)

IV : 86

When a (courteous) greeting
Is offered you, meet it
With a greeting still more
Courteous, or (at least)
Of equal courtesy.
God takes careful account [34]
Of all things.

HAVE MUTUAL CONSULTATION

XLII : 36 to 39

36. Whatever ye are given (here)
Is (but) a convenience [35]

34. The necessary correlative to the command to fight in a good cause is the command to cultivate sweetness and cordiality in our manners at all times. For fighting is an exceptional necessity, while the sweetness of daily human intercourse is a normal need. Further, we give kindness and courtesy without asking, and return it if possible in even better terms than we received, or at least in equally courteous terms. For we are all creatures of one God, and shall be brought together before Him.

35. Any good (or ill) which is our lot is only a temporary phase to serve the convenience of this life. But there is a

Of this Life : but that
Which is with God
Is better and more lasting :
(It is) for those who believe [36]
And put their trust
In their Lord ;
37. Those who avoid the greater [37]
Crimes and shameful deeds,
And, when they are angry
Even then forgive ;
38. Those who hearken [38]
To their Lord, and establish

higher good, which comes from God's own Presence. Such good is both superior in quality, and more permanent. In the same way, any ills that we may suffer in this life, have reference only to the conditions of this our life of probation. The ills that we "earn" in our spiritual Life—such as deprivation of God's Grace—are far more momentous and permanent.

36. The higher and more permanent gifts which come from God's Presence are for those who truly worship and serve God. These are described by nine of their characteristics, *viz.* : (1) they have Faith ; and it follows that (2) they trust in God, instead of running after false standards or values ; (3) they eschew the more serious offences against God's Law, and of course keep clear of any offences against sex ("shameful deeds") ; (4) while knowing that they are not themselves perfect, they are ready to forgive others, even though they are sorely tried with anger and provocation ; for the rest see n. 38.

37. Here we are speaking of the ordinary man or woman who tries to follow God's Law : he or she is not perfect, but at least eschews the major breaches of conduct. For those higher in spiritual degree there is of course a stricter standard. But all are entitled to the blessing of Islam, whatever their degree.

38. Continuing the enumeration of characteristics described in n. 36 above, we have the following further qualities in those who wish to serve God. (5) They are ready at all times to hearken to God's Signs, or to listen to the admonitions of men of God, and to follow the true Path, as they understand it; (6) they keep personal contact with God, by habits of Prayer

Regular prayer ; who (conduct)
Their affairs by mutual Consultation ; [39]
Who spend out of what
We bestow on them
For Sustenance ;

39. And those who, when
An oppressive wrong is inflicted
On them (are not cowed
But), help and defend themselves.

HUMILIATE, ETC.

XXV : 63 to 68

63. And the servants of (God)
Most Gracious are those

and Praise ; (7) their conduct in life is open and determined by mutual Consultation between those who are entitled to a voice, *e.g.*, in private domestic affairs, as between husband and wife, or other responsible members of the household ; in affairs of business, as between partners or parties interested ; and in state affairs as between rulers and ruled, or as between different departments of administration, to preserve the unity of administration ; (8) they do not forget Charity or the help due to their weaker brethren, out of the wealth or gifts or talents or opportunities, which God has provided for themselves ; and (9) when other people use them despitefully, they are not cowed down or terrorised into submission and acceptance of evil, but stand up for their rights.

39. '*Consultation*.' This is the key-word of the Sura, and suggests the ideal way in which a good man should conduct his affairs, so that, on the one hand, he may not become too egotistical, and, on the other, he may not lightly abandon the responsibilities which devolve on him as a Personality whose development counts in the sight of God. See the points in head (7) under n. 38 above. This principle was applied to its fullest extent by the holy Prophet in his private and public life, and was fully acted upon by the early rulers of Islam. Modern representative Government is an attempt—by no means perfect —to apply this principle in State affairs.

Who walk on the earth
In humility, and when the ignorant [40]
Address them, they say,
" Peace ! " ;
64. Those who spend the night
In adoration of their Lord
Prostrate and standing ; [41]
65. Those who say, " Our Lord ! "
Avert from us the Wrath
Of Hell, for its Wrath
Is indeed an affliction grievous,— [42]
66. " Evil indeed is it
As an abode, and as
A place to rest in " ; [43]
67. Those who, when they spend,
Are not extravagant and not
Niggardly, but hold a just (balance)
Between those (extremes) ; [44]

40. *Ignorant* : in a spiritual sense. *Address* : in the agressive nse. Their humility is shown in two ways : (1) to those in al search of knowledge, they give such knowledge as they ive and as the recipients can assimilate ; (2) to those who erely dispute, they do not speak harshly, but say " peace ! ", as uch as to say, " May it be well with you, may you repent and better " ; or " May God give me peace from such wrangling " ; " peace, and Good-bye ; let me leave you ! "

41. Humble prayer brings them nearer to God.

42. This is a prayer of humility : such a person relies, not on y good works which he may have done, but on the Grace and ercy of God ; and he shows a lively sense of the Day of Judg- ent, when every action will weigh for or against a soul.

43. The misery which results from sin is not only grievous live in (" an abode ") but also grievous " to rest in " or " to and in ", if it be only for a short time.

44. In ordinary spending this is a wise rule. But even in arity, in which we give of our best, it is not expected that should be extravagant, *i.e.*, that we should either do it for

68. Those who invoke not,
With God, any other god,
Nor slay such life as God
Has made sacred, except
For just cause, nor commit[45]
Fornication ;—and any that does
This (not only) meets punishment,

HELP IN PIETY

V : 3 (part)

Help ye one another
In righteousness and piety,
But help ye not one another
In sin and enmity :
Fear God : for God
Is strict in punishment.

show, to impress other people, or do it thoughtlessly, which would be the case if we "rob Peter to pay Paul". We should certainly not be niggardly, but we should remember every one's rights, including our own, and strike a perfectly just balance between them.

45. Here three things are expressly condemned : (1) false worship, which is a crime against God ; (2) the taking of life, which is a crime against our fellow-creatures ; and (3) fornication, which is a crime against our self-respect, against ourselves. Every crime is against God, His creatures, and ourselves, but some may be viewed more in relation to one than to another. The prohibition against taking life is qualified : "except for just cause" : *e.g.*, in judicial punishment for murder, or in self-preservation, which may include not only self-defence in the legal sense, but also the clearing out of pests, and the provision of meat under conditions of *Halal*.

JUST MEASURE

XXVI : 181 to 183

181. " Give just measure,[46]
And cause no loss
(To others by fraud).
182. " And weigh with scales
True and upright.
183. " And withhold not things
Justly due to men,
Nor do evil in the land,
Working mischief.

JUSTICE

IV : 58

God doth command you
To render back your Trusts
To those to whom they are due ;
And when ye judge
Between man and man
That ye judge with justice :
Verily how excellent
Is the teaching which He giveth you !
For God is He Who heareth
And seeth all things.

46. They were a commercial people, but they were given to fraud, injustice, and wrongful mischief (by intermeddling with others). They are asked to fear God and follow His ways : it is He Who also created their predecessors among mankind, who never prospered by fraud and violent wrong-doing, but only by justice and fair dealing.

IV : 135

O ye who believe !
Stand out firmly
For justice, as witnesses [47]
To God, even as against
Yourselves, or your parents,
Or your kin, and whether
It be (against) rich or poor : [48]
For God can best protect both.
Follow not the lusts
Of your hearts, lest ye
Swerve, and if ye
Distort (justice) or decline
To do justice, verily
God is well acquainted
With all that ye do.

V : 9

O ye who believe !
Stand out firmly

47. Justice is God's attribute, and to stand firm for justice is to be a witness to God, even if it is detrimental to our own interests (as we conceive them) or the interests of those who are near and dear to us. According to the Latin saying, "Let justice be done though heaven should fall".

But Islamic justice is something higher than the formal justice of Roman Law or any other human Law. It is even more penetrative than the subtler justice in the speculations of the Greek Philosophers. It searches out the innermost motives, because we are to act as in the presence of God, to whom all things, acts, and motives are known.

48. Some people may be inclined to favour the rich, because they expect something from them. Some people may be inclined to favour the poor because they are generally helpless. Partiality

For God, as witnesses
To fair dealing, and let not
The hatred of others
To you make you swerve[49]
To wrong and depart from
Justice. Be just: that is
Next to Piety: and fear God.
For God is well-acquainted
With all that ye do.

V : 14

But because of their breach
of their Covenant, We
Cursed them,[50] and made
Their hearts grow hard:
They change the words
From their (right) places
And forget a good part
Of the Message that was

in either case is wrong. Be just, without fear or favour. Both the rich and the poor are under God's protection as far as their legitimate interests are concerned, but they cannot expect to be favoured at the expense of others. And He can protect their interests far better than any man.

49. To do justice and act righteously in a favourable or neutral atmosphere is meritorious enough, but the real test comes when you have to do justice to people who hate you or to whom you have an aversion. But no less is required of you by the higher moral law.

50. *Cursed them*: that means that because of the breach of their Covenant, God withdrew His overflowing Grace from them. The withdrawal of Grace made their hearts grow hard in two ways: (1) they were no longer protected from the assaults of evil, and (2) they became impervious even to the message of forgiveness any mercy which is open to all God's creatures.

Sent them, nor wilt thou
Cease to find them—
Barring a few—ever
Bent on (new) deceits:[51]
But forgive them, and overlook
(Their misdeeds): for God
Loveth those who are kind.

XVI : 90

God commands justice, the doing of
good, and liberality to kith
And kin, and He forbids
All shameful deeds, and injustice
And rebellion: He instructs you,
That ye may receive admonition.[52]

KIND WORDS

II: 263

Kind words[53]
And the covering of faults

51. Israel, when it lost God's grace as above, began to sin against truth and religion in three ways: (1) they began to misuse Scripture itself, by either taking words out of their right meaning, or applying them to things for which they were never meant; (2) in doing so they conveniently forgot a part of the Message and purpose of God; and (3) they invented new deceits and go on doing it to support the old ones.

52. Justice is a comprehensive term, and may include all the virtues of cold philosophy. But religion asks for something warmer and more human, the doing of good deeds even where perhaps they are not strictly demanded by justice, such as returning good for ill, or obliging those who in worldly language "have no claim" on you; and of course *à fortiori* the fulfilling of the claims of those whose claims are recognized in social life. Similarly the opposites are to be avoided: everything that is recognized as shameful, and everything that is really unjust, and any inward rebellion against God's Law of our own conscience in its most sensitive form.

53. A very high standard is set for charity. (1) It must be in

Are better than charity
Followed by injury.
God is Free of all wants,
And He is most Forbearing.

MAKE BEQUESTS

II : 180

It is prescribed,
When death approaches
Any of you, if he leave
Any goods, that he make a bequest
To parents and next of kin,[54]
According to reasonable usage;
This is due
From the God-fearing.

the way of God. (2) It must expect no reward in this world. (3) It must not be followed by references or reminders to the act of charity. (4) Still less should any annoyance or injury be caused to the recepient, *e.g.*, by boasting that the giver relieved the person in the hour of need. Indeed the kindness and the spirit which turns a blind eye to other people's faults or short-comings is the essence of charity: these things are better than charity if charity is spoilt by tricks that do harm. At the same time, while no reward is to be *expected*, there is abundant reward from God—material, moral, and spiritual – according to His own good pleasure and plan. If we spend in the way of God, it is not as if God was in need of our charity. On the contrary our shortcomings are so great that we require His utmost forbearance before any good that we can do can merit His praise or reward. Our motives are so mixed that our best may really be very poor if judged by a very strict standard.

54. There are rules of course for the disposal of intestate property. But it is a good thing that a dying man or woman should, of his own free-will, think of his parents and his next of kin, not in a spirit of injustice to others, but in a spirit of love and reverence for those who have cherished him. He must, however, do it "according to reasonable usage."

PIETY

XXII : 37

It is not their meat
Nor their blood, that reaches
God : it is your piety
That reaches Him : He
Has thus made them subject
To you, that ye may
Glorify God for His guidance : [55]
And Proclaim the Good News
To all who do right.

QISAS

II : 178 and 179

178. O ye who believe !
The law of equality : [56]

55. No one should suppose that meat or blood is acceptable to the One True God. It was a pagan fancy that God could be appeased by blood sacrifice. But God does accept the offering of our hearts, and as a symbol of such offer, some visible institution is necessary. He has given us power over the brute creation, and permitted us to eat meat, but only if we pronounce His name at the solemn act of taking life, for without this solemn invocation, we are apt to forget the sacredness of life. By the invocation we are reminded that wanton cruetly is not in our thoughts, but only the need of food. Now if we further deny ourselves the greater part of the food (some theologians fix the proportion at three-quarters or two-thirds) for the sake of our poorer brethren in solemn assembly in the precincts of the *Haram* (Sacred territory), our symbolic act finds practical expression in benevolence, and that is the virtue sought to be taught. We should be grateful to God for His guidance in this matter, in which many Peoples have gone wrong, and we should proclaim the true doctrine, so that virtue and charity may increase among men.

56. Note first that this verse and the next make it clear that Islam has much mitigated the horrors of the pre-Islamic custom

Is prescribed to you
In cases of murder :[57]
The free for the free,
The slave for the slave,
The woman for the woman.
But if any remission
Is made by the brother[58]
Of the slain, then grant

of retaliation. In order to meet the strict claims of justice, equality is prescribed, with a strong recommendation for mercy and forgiveness. To translate '*Qisas*', therefore, by retaliation, is I think, incorrect. The Latin legal term *Lex Talionis* may come near it, but even that is modified here. In any case it is best to avoid technical terms for things that are very different. 'Retaliation' in English has a wider meaning, equivalent almost to returning evil for evil, and would more fitly apply to the blood feuds of the Days of Ignorance. Islam says : if you *must* take a life for a life, at least there should be some measure of equality in it ; the killing of the slave of a tribe should not involve a blood-feud where many free men would be killed ; but the law of Mercy, where it can be obtained by consent, with reasonable compensation, would be better.

Our law of equality only takes account of three conditions in civil society; free for free, slave for slave, woman for woman. Among free men or women, all are equal : you cannot ask that because a wealthy, or high-born, or influential man is killed, his life is equal to two or three lives among the poor or the lowly. Nor, in cases of murder, can you go into the value or abilities of a slave. A woman is mentioned separately because her position as a mother or an economic worker is different. She does not form a third class, but a division in the other two classes. One life having been lost, do not waste many lives in retaliation ; at most, let the Law take one life under strictly prescribed conditions, and shut the door to private vengeance or tribal retaliation. But if the aggrieved party consents (and this condition of consent is laid down to prevent worse evils), forgiveness and brotherly love is better, and the door of Mercy is kept open. In Western law, no felony can be compounded.

57. The jurists have carefully laid down that the law of *qisas* refers to murder only. *Qisas* is not applicable to manslaughter, due to a mistake or an accident. There, there would be no capital punishment.

58. *The brother* : the term is perfectly general ; all men are brothers in Islam. In this, and in all questions of inheritance,

Any reasonable demand,[59]
And compensate him
With handsome gratitude.
This is a concession
And a Mercy
From your Lord.
After this whoever
Exceeds the limits
Shall be in grave penalty.
179. In the Law of Equality
There is (saving of) Life
To you, O ye men of understanding;
That ye may
Restrain yourselves.

REPENTANCE

IV : 17 and 18

17. God accepts the repentance
Of those who do evil

females have similar rights to males, and therefore the masculine gender imports both sexes. Here we are considering the rights of the heirs in the light of the larger brotherhood. In 178-79 we have the rights of the heirs to life.

59. The demand should be such as can be met by the party concerned, *i.e.*, within his means, and reasonable according to justice and good conscience. For example, a demand could not be made affecting the honour of a woman or a man. The whole penalty can be remitted if the aggrieved party agrees, out of brotherly love. In meeting that demand the culprit or his friends should equally be generous and recognize the good-will of the other side. There should be no subterfuges, no bribes, no unseemly bye-play : otherwise the whole intention of mercy and peace is lost.

In ignorance and repent
Soon afterwards ; to them
Will God turn in mercy :
For God is full of knowledge
And wisdom.
18. Of no effect is the repentance
Of those who continue[60]
To do evil, until Death
Faces one of them, and he says,
" Now have I repented indeed ; "
Nor of those who die
Rejecting Faith : for them
Have we prepared
A punishment most grievous.

RIGHT (ENJOINING)

III : 110 (part)

Ye are the best
Of Peoples, evolved
For mankind,
Enjoining what is right,
Forbidding what is wrong,
And believing in God.[61]

60. Note the fine touch. A sin may be fashionable, and people sin together without compunction. When one of them is faced with Death, he repents, but that sort of repentance is no good.

61. The logical conclusion to the evolution of religious history is a non-sectarian, non-racial, non-doctrinal, universal religion, which Islam claims to be. For Islam is just submission to the Will of God. This implies (1) Faith, (2) doing right, being an example to others to do right, and having the power to see that the right prevails, (3) eschewing wrong, being an example to others to eschew wrong, and having the power

RECOMMEND GOOD CAUSE

IV : 85

Whoever recommends
And helps a good cause
Becomes a partner therein :
And whoever recommends
And helps an evil cause,
Shares in its burden :
And God hath power [62]
Over all things.

REPEL EVIL

XXIII : 96

Repel evil with that [63]
Which is best : We are

to see that wrong and injustice are defeated. Islam therefore lives, not for itself, but for mankind. The People of the Book, if only they had faith would be Muslims for they have been prepared for Islam. Unfortunately there is Unfaith, but it can never harm those who carry the banner of Faith and Right, which must always be victorious.

62. In this fleeting world's chances God's providence and justice may not always appear plain to our eyes. But we are asked to believe that if we help and support a good cause, we share in all its credit and in its eventual victory. And conversely, we cannot support a bad cause without sharing in all its evil consequences. If appearances seem against this faith, let us not be deceived by appearances. For God has power over all things.

63. Whether people speak evil of you, in your presence or behind your back, or they do evil to you in either of those ways, all is known to God. It is not for you to punish. Your best course is not to do evil in your turn, but to do what will best repel the evil. Two evils do not make a good.

Well acquainted with
The things they say.

SCRIBE TRANSACTIONS

II : 282 and 283

282. O ye who believe!
When ye deal with each other,
In transactions involving
Future obligations
In a fixed period of time,
Reduce them to writing.[64]
Let a scribe write down
Faithfully as between
The parties : let not the scribe
Refuse to write: as God[65]
Has taught him,
So let him write.

64. The first part of the verse deals with transactions involving future payment or future consideration, and the second part with transactions in which payment and delivery are made on the spot. Examples of the former are if goods are bought now and payment is promised at a fixed time and place in the future, or if cash is paid now and delivery is contracted for at a fixed time and place in the future. In such cases a written document is recommended, but it is held that the words later on in this verse, that it is "juster...more suitable as evidence, and more convenient to prevent doubts," etc., imply that it is not obligatory in law. Examples of the latter kind—cash payment and delivery on the spot—require no evidence in writing, but apparently oral witnesses to such transactions are recommended.

65. The scribe in such matters assumes a fiduciary capacity : he should, therefore, remember to act as in the presence of God, with full justice to both parties. The art of writing he should look upon as a gift from God and he should use it as in His service. In an illiterate population the scribe's position is still more responsible.

Let him who incurs
The liability dictate,
But let him fear
His Lord God,
And not diminish
Aught of what he owes.
If the party liable
Is mentally deficient,
Or weak, or unable
Himself to dictate,[66]
Let his guardian
Dictate faithfully.
And get two witnesses,
Out of your own men,[67]
And if there are not two men,
Then a man and two women,
Such as ye choose,
For witnesses,
So that if one of them errs,
The other can remind her.
The witnesses
Should not refuse
When they are called on
(For evidence).
Disdain not to reduce
To writing (your contract)

66. Possibly the person " mentally deficient, or weak or unable to dictate," may also be incapable of making a valid contract, and the whole duty would be on his guardian, who again must act in perfect good faith, not only protecting but vigilently promoting the interests of his ward.

67. It is desirable that the men(or women) who are chosen as witnesses should be from the circle to which the parties belong, as they would best be able to understand the transaction, and be most easily available if their evidence is required in future.

For a future period,
Whether it be small
Or big : it is juster
In the sight of God,
More suitable as evidence.
And more convenient
To prevent doubts
Among yourselves.
But if it be a transaction
Which ye carry out
On the spot among yourselves,
There is no blame on you
If ye reduce it not
To writing.
But take witnesses
Whenever ye make
A commercial contract ,
And let neither scribe
Nor witness suffer harm
If ye do (such harm),
It would be wickedness
In you. So fear God ,
For it is God
That teaches you.
And God is well-acquainted
With all things.[68]

283 If ye are on a journey,
And cannot find a scribe, a pledge

68 Commercial morality is here taught on the highest plane and yet in the most practical manner, both as regards the bargains to be made, the evidence to be provided, the doubts to be avoided, and the duties and rights of scribes and witnesses. Probity even in worldly matters is to be, not a mere matter of convenience or policy, but a matter of conscience and religious duty. Even our every-day transactions are to be carried out as in the presence of God.

With possession (may serve
The purpose).[69]
And if one of you
Deposits a thing
On trust with another,[70]
Let the trustee
(Faithfully) discharge
His trust, and let him
Fear His Lord.
Conceal not evidence ;
For whoever conceals it,—
His heart is tainted[71]
With sin. And God
Knoweth all that ye do.

69. A pledge or security stands on its own independent footing, though it is a very convenient form of closing the bargain where the parties cannot trust each other, and cannot get a written agreement with proper witnesses.

70. The law of deposit implies great trust in the Depositary on the part of the Depositor. The Depositary becomes a trustee, and the doctrine of Trust can be further developed on that basis. The trustee's duty is to guard the interests of the person on whose behalf he holds the trust and to render back the property and accounts when required according to the terms of the trust. This duty again is linked to the sanction of Religion, which requires a higher standard than Law.

71. It sometimes happens that if some inconvenient piece of evidence is destroyed or concealed, we gain a great advantage materially. We are warned not to yield to such a temptation. The concealment of evidence has a serious effect on our own moral and spiritual life, for it taints the very source of higher life, as typified by the heart. The heart is also the seat of our secrets. We are told that the sin will reach our most secret being, though the sin may not be visible or open to the world. Further the heart is the seat of our affections, and false dealing taints all our affections.

SPEAK FAIR

XVII : 53

Say to My servants
That they should (only) say
Those things that are best:[72]
For Satan doth sow
Dissensions among them:
For Satan is to man
An avowed enemy.

SELF-RESTRAINT

XLI : 34 and 35

34. Nor can Goodness and Evil[73]
Be equal. Repel (Evil)
With what is better:
Then will he between whom

72. This command refers to two situations. (1) Even to your enemies and the enemies of God you should speak fair: who are you to judge others? Judgment belongs to God alone, for He knows you (*i.e.*, all mankind) best, and your personal knowledge is at best imperfect. And Satan is always trying to divide mankind. (2) Amongst yourselves, also, you should not entertain suspicions, but speak politely according to the best standards of human speech. A false or unkind word may destroy all your efforts at building up unity, because the forces of disruption are more numerous than the forces of unity.

73. You do not *return* good for evil, for there is no equality or comparison between the two. You repel or destroy evil with something which is far better, just as an antidote is better than poison. You foil hatred with love. You repel ignorance with knowledge, folly and wickedness with the friendly message of Revelation. The man who was in the bondage of sin, you not only liberate from sin, but make him your greatest friend and helper in the cause of God! Such is the alchemy of the Word of God!

And thee was hatred
Become as it were
Thy friend and intimate !
35 And no one will be[74]
Granted such goodness
Except those who exercise
Patience and self-restraint,—
None but persons of
The greatest good fortune.

TRADE

IV : 29 to 31

29. O ye who believe ![75]

74. The moral standard referred to in the last verse can only be reached by the exercise of the highest patience and self-restraint. All sorts of human weaknesses and counsels of pseudo wisdom and "self respect" will keep breaking in, but resist them as suggestions of Evil. If you can reach anywhere near that high standard, you will be indeed most fortunate in a spiritual sense, for God's Revelation will have made you great and free.

75 Let me paraphrase this verse for there is profound meaning in it. (1) All your property you hold in trust, whether it is in your name, or belongs to the community, or to people over whom you have control. To waste is wrong. (2) In II. 188 the same phrase occurred, to caution us against greed. Here it occurs, to encourage us to increase property by economic use (traffic and trade), recalling Christ's parable of the Talents (Matt. XXV. 14-30), where the servants who had increased their master's wealth were promoted and the servant who had hoarded was cast into darkness. (3) We are warned that our waste may mean our own destruction ("nor kill or destroy yourselves"). But there is a more general meaning also : we must be careful of our own and other people's lives. We must commit no violence. This is the opposite of "trade and traffic by mutual good-will". (4) Our violence to our own brethren is particularly preposterous, seeing that God has loved and showered His mercies on us and all His creatures.

Eat not up your property
Among yourselves in vanities:
But let there be amongst you
Traffic and trade
By mutual good-will:
Nor kill (or destroy)
Yourselves: for verily
God hath been to you
Most Merciful!

30. If any do that
In rancour and injustice,—
Soon shall We scorch them
In the Fire: and easy
It is for God.

31. If ye but eschew
The most heinous
Of the things
Which ye are forbidden to do,
We shall expel
Out of you
All the evil in you,
And admit you to a Gate
Of great honour.

UNITY

III: 103 (part)

And hold fast,
All together, by the Rope[76]

76. The simile is that of people struggling in deep water, to whom a benevolent Providence stretches out a strong and unbreakable rope of rescue. If all hold fast to it together, their mutual support adds to the chance of their safety.

Which God (stretches out
For you), and be not divided
Among yourselves ;

IX : 71

The Believers, men
And women, are protectors,
One of another : they enjoin
What is just, and forbid
What is evil : they observe
Regular prayers, practise
Regular charity, and obey
God and His Apostle.
On them will God pour
His mercy : for God
Is Exalted in Power, Wise.

XLIX : 9 and 10

9. If two parties among[77]
The Believers fall into
A quarrel, make ye peace
Between them : but if
One of them transgresses
Beyond bounds against the other,

77. Individual quarrels are easier to compose than group quarrels, or, in the modern world, national quarrels. But the collective community of Islam should be supreme over groups or nations. It would be expected to act justly and try to compose the quarrel, for peace is better than fighting. But if one party is determined to be the aggressor, the whole force of the community is brought to bear on it. The essential condition of course is that there should be perfect fairness and justice and respect for the highest principles, for Islam takes account of every just and legitimate interest without separating spiritual from temporal matters. The League of Nations fails because these essentials are absent.

Then fight ye (all) against
The one that transgresses
Until it complies with
The command of God;
But if it complies, then
Make peace between them
With justice, and be fair:
For God loves those
Who are fair (and just).
10. The Believers are but
A single Brotherhood:[78]
So make peace and
Reconciliation between your
Two (contending) brothers;
And fear God that ye
May receive mercy.

VIRTUES TO BE FOLLOWED

XXXIII : 35

For Muslim men and women,—[79]
For believing men and women,
For devout men and women,
For true men and women,
For men and women who are
Patient and constant, for men
And women who humble themselves,

78. The enforcement of the Muslim Brotherhood is the greatest social ideal of Islam. On it was based the Prophet's Sermon at his last pilgrimage, and Islam cannot be completely realised until this ideal is achieved.

79. Islam, or submitting our will to God's Will, includes all the virtues, as particularly specified in this Verse.

For men and women who give[80]
In charity, for men and women
Who fast (and deny themselves),
For men and women who
Guard their chastity, and
For men and women who
Engage much in God's praise,—[81]
For them has God prepared
Forgiveness and great reward.

---

80. A number of Muslim virtues are specified here, but the chief stress is laid on the fact that these virtues are as necessary to women as to men. Both sexes have spiritual as well as human rights and duties in an equal degree, and the future " reward " of the Hereafter. *viz* , Spiritual Bliss is provided for the one as for the other.

81. The virtues referred to are : (1) Faith, hope, and trust in God, and in His benevolent government of the world; (2) devotion and service in practical life ; (3) love and practice of truth, in thought and intention, word and deed ; (4) patience and constancy, in suffering and in right endeavour ; (5) humility, the avoidance of an attitude of arrogance and superiority ; (6) charity, *i.e.*, help to the poor and unfortunate ones in life, a special virtue arising out of the general duty of service ; No. (2) ; (7) self-denial, typically in food, but generally in all appetites ; (8) chastity, purity in sex life, purity in motive, thought, word, and deed ; and (9) constant attention to God's Message, and cultivation of the desire to get nearer to God.

II.—ALLAH FORBIDS

ADULTERY

XVII : 32

Nor come nigh to adultery :
For it is a shameful (deed)
And an evil, opening the road[82]
(To other evils)

XXIV : 2

The woman and the man
Guilty of adultery or fornication,—[83]
Flog each of them
With a hundred stripes :
Let not compassion move you
In their case, in a matter

82. Literally. " It is evil as a road (or a way) Adultery is not only shameful in itself and inconsistent with any self-respect or respect for others, but it opens the road to many evils. It destroys the basis of the family ; it works against the interests of children born or to be born ; it may cause murders and feuds and loss of reputation and property, and also loosen permanently the bonds of society. Not only should it be avoided as a sin, but any approach or temptation to it should be avoided.

83. *Zina* includes sexual intercourse between a man and a woman not married to each other. It therefore applies both to adultery (which implies that one or both of the parties are married to a person or persons other than the ones concerned) and to fornication, which, in its strict signification, implies that both parties are unmarried. The law of marriage and divorce is made easy in Islam, so that there may be the less temptation

Prescribed by God, if ye believe
In God and the Last Day :
And let a party
Of the Believers
Witness their punishment.[84]

BRIBERY

II : 188

And do not eat up
Your property among yourselves
For vanities, nor use it
As bait for the judges,
With intent that ye may
Eat up wrongfully and knowingly
A little of (other) people's property.[85]

for intercourse outside the well-defined incidents of marriage. This makes for greater self-respect for both man and woman. Other sex offences are also punishable, but this Section applies strictly to *Zina* as above defined.

84. The punishment should be open, in order to be deterrent.

85. Besides the three primal physical needs of man, which are apt to make him greedy, there is a fourth greed in society, the greed of wealth and property. The purpose of fasts is not completed until this fourth greed is also restrained. Ordinarily honest men are content if they refrain from robbery, theft, or embezzlement. Two more subtle forms of the greed are mentioned here. One is where one uses one's own property fo corrupting others—judges or those in authority—so as to obtain some material gain even under the cover and protection of the law. The words translated "other people's property" may also mean "public property". A still more subtle form is where we use our own property or property under our own control—"among yourselves" in the Text—for vain or frivolous uses. Under the Islamic standard this is also greed. Property carries with it its own responsibilities. If we fail to understand or fulfil them we have not learnt the full lesson of self-denial by fasts.

COVETOUSNESS

IV : 32

And in no wise covet [86]
Those things in which God
Hath bestowed His gifts
More freely on some of you
Than on others : to men
Is allotted what they earn,
And to women what they earn :
But ask God of His bounty.
For God hath full knowledge
Of all things.

SECTARIANISM

VI : 159

As for those who divide [87]
Their religion and break up

86. Men and women have gifts from God—some greater than others. They seem unequal, but we are assured that Providence has allotted them by a scheme by which people receive what they earn. If this does not appear clear in our sight, let us remember that we have no full knowledge but God has. We must not be jealous if other people have more than we have—in wealth or position or strength or honour or talent or happiness.

Probably things are equalized in the aggregate or in the long run, or equated to needs and merits on a scale which we cannot appraise. If we want more, instead of being jealous or covetous, we should pray to God and place before Him our needs. Though He knows all, and has no need of our prayer, our prayer may reveal to ourselves our shortcomings and enable us to deserve more of God's bounty or make ourselves fit for it.

87. *Divide their religion* : *Farraqu* : *i.e.*, (1) make a distinction between one part of it and another, take the part which suits them

Into sects, thou hast
No part in them in the least:
Their affair is with God:
He will in the end
Tell them the truth
Of all that they did.

DISPUTE IN BOOK

II : 174 to 176

174 Those who conceal
God's revelations in the Book,
And purchase for them
A miserable profit,—
They swallow into themselves [88]
Naught but Fire;

and reject the rest; or (2) have religion one day of the week and the world the rest of the six days; or (3) keep "religion in its right place," as if it did not claim to govern the whole life; make a sharp distinction between the secular and the religious; or (4) show a sectarian bias, seek differences in views, so as to break up the unity of Islam.

88. "They eat nothing but fire into their bellies" is a literal translation that produces an effect of rude inelegance which is not in the Arabic words. Even in the matter of food and drinks, the mission of Islam is to avoid the extremes of lawlessness on the one hand and extreme formalism on the other. It has laid down a few simple and very reasonable rules. Their infraction causes loss of health or physical powers in any case. But if there is further a spirit of subjective rebellion or fraud—passing off in the name of religion something which is far from the purpose.—the consequences become also moral and spiritual. Then it becomes a sin against Faith and Spirit. Continuing the physical simile, we actually swallow fire into ourselves. Imagine the torments which we would have if we swallowed fire into our physical body! They would be infinitely worse in our spiritual state, and they would go on to the Day of Resurrection, when we shall be deprived even of the words which the Judge speaks to a reasonable culprit, and we shall certainly not win His Grace and Mercy.

God will not address them
On the Day of Resurrection,
Nor purify them :
Grievous will be
Their Penalty.
175. They are the ones
Who buy Error
in place of Guidance
And Torment in place
Of Forgiveness.
Ah ! what boldness
(They show) for the Fire !
176. (Their doom is) because
God sent down the Book
In truth but those who seek
Causes of dispute in the Book
Are in a schism [89]
Far (from the purpose)

EATING UP ORPHAN'S PROPERTY

IV : 2

To orphans restore their property
(When they reach their age),
Nor substitute (your) worthless things
For (their) good ones ; and devour not

89. From the mere physical regulation we are at once lifted up into the sphere of morals and faith. For the one acts and reacts on the other. If we are constantly carping at wholesome regulations, we shall do nothing but cause division and schisms among the people, and ordered society would tend to break up.

Their substance (by mixing it up)[90]
With your own. For this is
Indeed a great sin.

IV : 10

Those who unjustly
Eat up the property
Of orphans, eat up
A Fire into their own
Bodies : they will soon
Be enduring a blazing Fire !

VI : 152

And come not nigh
To the orphan's property,
Except to improve it,
Until he attain the age
Of full strength ; give measure
And weight with (full) justice ;—
No burden do We place
On any soul, but that
Which it can bear ;—
Whatever ye say, speak justly,
Even if a near relative
Is concerned ; and fulfil

90. Justice to orphans is enjoined, and three things are particularly mentioned as temptations in the way of a guardian : (1) He must not postpone restoring all his ward's property when the time comes. (2) If there is a list of property, it is not enough that that list should be technically followed ; the property restored must be of equal value to the property received, the same principle applies where there is no list. (3) If property is managed together or where perishable goods must necessarily be consumed, the strictest probity is necessary when the separation takes place and this is insisted on.

The Covenant of God:
Thus doth He command you,
That ye may remember.

EXTRAVAGANCE

II : 143 (part)

Thus [91] have We made of you
An *Ummat* justly balanced,[92]
That ye might be witnesses [93]
As between the nations,
And the Apostle a witness
As between yourselves.

91. *Thus* : By giving you a Qibla of your own, most ancient in history, and most modern as a symbol of your organization as a new nation (*Ummat*).

92. *Justly balanced* : The essence of Islam is to avoid all extravagances on either side. It is a sober, practical religion. But the Arabic word (*wasat*) also implies a touch of the literal meaning of intermediacy. Geographically Arabia is in an intermediate position in the Old World, as was proved in history by the rapid expansion of Islam, North, South, West and East.

93. *Witnesses*: When two persons dispute, they advance extravagant claims. A just witness comes between them, and brings the light of reason to bear on them, pruning all their selfish extravagances So the mission of Islam is to curb, for instance, the extreme formalism of the Mosaic law and the extreme "other worldliness" professed by Christianity. The witness must be unselfish, equipped with first-hand knowledge and ready to intervene in the cause of justice. Such is the position claimed by Islam among rival systems. Similarly, within Islam itself, the position of witness to whom disputants can appeal is held by Muhammad Mustafa.

XVII : 26 and 27

26. And render to the kindred
Their due rights, as (also)
To those in want,
And to the Wayfarer[94]
But squander not (your wealth)
In the manner of a spendthrift.[95]
27. Verily spendthrifts are brothers
Of the Evil Ones;
And the Evil One
Is to his Lord (Himself)
Ungrateful[96]

EXULTATION

XXVIII : 76 (part)

" Exult not, for God loveth not
Those who exult (in riches).

94. In the Jewish Decalogue, which was given to a primitive and hard hearted people, this refinement of kindness,—to those in want and to wayfarers (*i.e.*, total strangers whom you come across) finds no place. Nor was there much danger of their wasting their substance out of exuberance. Even the command "to honour thy father and mother" comes after the ceremonial observance of the Sabbath. With us, the worship of God is linked up with kindness—to parents, kindred, those in want, those who are far from their homes though they may be total strangers to us. It is not mere verbal kindness. They have certain rights which must be fulfilled.

95. All charity, kindness and help are conditioned by our own resources. There is no merit if we merely spend out of bravado or for idle show. How many families are ruined by extravagant expenses at weddings, funerals, etc., or (as they may call it) to "oblige friends or relatives," or to give to able-bodied beggars? To no one was this command more necessary than to Muslims of the present day.

96. Spendthrifts are not merely fools. They are of the same family as the Evil Ones. And the chief of the Evil Ones (notice

FOLLOWING ONE'S OWN PASSIONS

XXV : 43

Seest thou such a one
As taketh for his god
His own passion (or impulse)?
Couldst thou be a disposer
Of affairs for him?[97]

HYPOCRISY

IV : 145 and 146

145. The hypocrites will be
In the lowest depths
Of the Fire: no helper
Wilt thou find for them;—
146. Except for those who repent,
Mend (their life), hold fast
To God, and purify their religion
As in God's sight: if so

the transition from the Plural to the Singular). Satan himself —fell by his ingratitude to God. So those who misuse or squander God's gifts are also ungrateful to God.

97. The man who worships his own passions or impluses or desires is the most hopeless to teach or lead or guide. If it were anything else the matter with him, the Teacher could argue with him. But Reason cannot prevail over blind passion. It is vain to hope that such a man could be led, until his mad desires are killed. No one could undertake any responsibility for him, for he obeys no law and follows no advice. He is worse than brute beasts, which may not understand, but at least follow the wholesome instincts implanted in them by God. The lawless man has killed his instincts and is unwilling to submit to guidance.

They will be (numbered) [98]
With the Believers.
And soon will God
Grant to the Believers
A reward of immense value.

IDLE CURIOSITY AND INSOLENCE

XVII: 36 and 37

36. And pursue not that
Of which thou hast [99]
No knowledge; for
Every act of hearing,
Or of seeing,
Or of (feeling in) the heart
Will be enquired into
(On the Day of Reckoning.)

98. Even hypocrites can obtain forgiveness, on four conditions: (1) sincere repentance, which purifies their minds; (2) amendment of their conduct, which purifies their outer life; (3) steadfastness and devotion to God, which strengthens their faith and protects them from the assaults of evil; and (4) sincerity in their religion, or their whole inner being, which brings them as full members into the goodly Fellowship of Faith.

99. Idle curiosity may lead us to nose into evil, through our ignorance that it is evil. We must guard against every such danger. We must only hear the things that are known to us to be of good report, and see things that are good and instructive, and entertain in our hearts feelings or in our minds ideas that we have reason to expect will be spiritually profitable to us. We shall be called to account for the exercise of every faculty that has been given to us. This goes a little farther than a famous sculpture on a Japanese temple in which three monkeys are shown as putting their hands to their ears, eyes, and mouths, respectively, to show that they were not prepared to hear any evil, or see any evil, or speak any evil. Here idle curiosity is condemned. Futility is to be avoided even if it does not reach the degree of positive evil.

37. Nor walk on the earth [100]
With insolence : for thou
Canst not rend the earth
Asunder, nor reach
The mountains in height.

PLOTTING OF EVIL

XXXV : 43 (part)

But the plotting of evil
Will hem in only
The authors thereof.

MISCHIEF

II : 60 (part)

So eat and drink
Of the sustenance provided by God,
And do no evil nor mischief
On the (face of the) earth.

II : 205 (part)

But God loveth not mischief

100. Insolence, or arrogance, or undue elation at our powers or capacities is the first step to many evils. Besides it is unjustified. All our gifts are from God.

V : 36

The punishment of those
Who wage war against God
And His Apostle, and strive
With might and main
For mischief through the land [101]
Is : execution, or crucifixion,
Or the cutting off of hands
And feet from Opposite sides,[102]
Or exile from the land :
That is their disgrace
In this world, and
A heavy punishment is theirs
In the Hereafter.

IX : 107 and 108

107. And there are those [103]
Who put up a mosque

101. For the double crime of treason against the State, combined with treason against God, as shown by overt crimes, four alternative punishments are mentioned, any one of which is to be applied according to circumstances : *viz.*, execution (cutting off of the head) crucifixion, maiming, or exile. These were features of the Criminal Law then and for centuries afterwards, except that tortures such as " hanging, drawing and quartering " in English Law, and piercing of eyes and leaving the unfortunate victim exposed to a tropical sun, which was practised in Arabia, and all such tortures were abolished. In any case sincere repentance before it was too late was recognized as a ground of mercy.

102. Understood to mean a hand and an arm from each side.

103. In this verse a class of insiduous evil-doers is mentioned whose type is illustrated in the story of the 'Qubaa' " Mosque of

By way of mischief and infidelity—
To disunite the Believers—
And in preparation for one [104]
Who warred against God
And His Apostle aforetime.
They will indeed swear
That their intention is nothing
But good ; but God doth declare
That they are certainly liars.
108. Never stand thou forth therein.
There is a mosque whose foundation [105]
Was laid from the first day
On piety ; it is more worthy
Of thy standing forth (for prayer)
Therein. In it are men who
Love to be purified ; and God
Loveth those who make themselves pure.

mischief " (*dhirar*). Qubaa is a suburb of Medina, about three miles to the south-east. When the Holy Prophet arrived at Medina for Hijrat, he rested four days in Qubaa before entering the town of Medina. Here was built the first mosque, the "Mosque of Piety" (*Taqwa*) or the mosque of the power of Islam (*Quwat-ul-Islam*), to which he frequently came during his subsequent stay in Medina. Taking advantage of these sacred associations, some Hypocrites, of the Tribe of Bani Ghanam built an opposition mosque in Qubba, pretending to advance Islam In reality they were in league with a notorious enemy of Islam, one Abu Amir, who had fought against Islam at Uhud and who was now, after the battle of Hunain (A.H. 9), in Syria ; his confederates wanted a mosque for him to come to but it would only be a source of mischief and division, and the scheme was disapproved.

104. Abu Amir, surnamed the *Rahib* (monk) as he had been in touch with Christian monks.

105. The original "Mosque of Piety" built by the Holy Apostle himself.

VII : 55 and 56

55. Call on your Lord
With humility and in private : [106]
For God loveth not
Those who trespass beyond bounds.
56. Do no mischief on the earth,
After it hath been [107]
Set in order, but call
On Him with fear [108]
And longing (in your hearts) :
For the Mercy of God
Is (always) near
To those who do right.

MISAPPROPRIATION

VIII : 27

O ye that believe !
Betray not the trust
Of God and the Apostle,
Nor misappropriate knowingly

106. In prayer, we must avoid any arrogance or show or loudness, or vanity of requests or words. If excess is condemned in all things, it is specially worthy of condemnation when we go humbly before our Lord,—we poor creatures before the Omnipotent Who knoweth all.

107. The man who prays with humility and earnestness finds the ground prepared by God for his spiritual advancement It is all set in order, and cleared of weeds. He does not, like the wicked, upset that order, to introduce evil or mischief into it.

108. *Fear and longing* : the fear of God is really a fear lest we should diverge from His Will, or do anything which would not be pleasing to Him : unlike ordinary fear, it therefore brings us nearer to God and in fact nourishes our longing and desire for Him.

Things entrusted to you.[109]

MURDER

IV : 93

If a man kills a Believer
Intentionally, his recompense [110]
Is Hell, to abide therein
(For ever) : and the wrath
And the curse of God
Are upon him, and
A dreadful penalty
Is prepared for him.

109. Trusts may be of various kinds : (1) property, goods, credit, etc. ; (2) plans, confidences, secrets, etc. ; (3) knowledge, talents, opportunities, etc., which we are expected to use for our fellowmen. Men may betray the trust of God and His Apostle by misusing property, or abusing the confidence reposed in them, or the knowledge or talents given to them. On that special occasion, when the plans for the protection of God's worshippers against annihilation were of special importance, the Apostle's trust and confidence had to be guarded with special care. Occasions for scrupulously respecting the trust and confidence of our fellow-men occur every day in our life, and few of us can claim perfection in this respect. Hence the special distinction of the man of God, who earned the title of *Al-Amin*, the one who was true to every trust reposed in him.

110. What is mentioned here is the punishment in the Hereafter, the spiritual consequences. The legal consequences, enforceable by human society, are mentioned in ii. 178, under the rules of *Qisas*. That is, a life should be taken for a life destroyed, but this should be on a scale of equality : a single murder should not commit a whole tribe to a perpetual blood-feud, as in the days of ignorance. But if the heirs of the man slain accept reasonable compensation, this should be accepted, and the taking of a life for a life should be put a stop to. This course leads to the saving of life, and is commanded to men of understanding.

XVII : 33

Nor take life—which God
Has made sacred—except
For just cause. And if
Anyone is slain wrongfully,
We have given his heir
Authority (to demand Qisas) [111]
(Or to forgive): but let him
Not exceed bounds in the matter
Of taking life; for he
Is helped (by the Law).

REVILING

VI : 108

Revile not ye
Those whom they call upon
Besides God, lest
They out of spite
Revile God
In their ignorance.
Thus have We made
Alluring to each people [112]

111. Under the strict limitations laid down, a life may be taken for a life. The heir is given the right to demand the life; but he must not exceed due bounds, because he is helped by the Law." Some Commentators understand "he" in "he is helped (by the Law)" to refer to the heir of the person against whom Qisas is sought. He too will be helped by the law, if the heir of the first slain exceeds the bounds of Law.

112. A man's actual personal religion depends upon many things,—his personal psychology, the background of his life, his hidden or repressed feelings, tendencies, or history (which

Its own doings.
In the end will they
Return to their Lord,
And We shall then
Tell them the truth
Of all that they did.

RIDICULE

XLIX : 11

O Ye who believe !
Let not some men

psycho-analysis tries to unravel), his hereditary dispositions or antipathies, and all the subtle influences of his education and his environment. The task before the man of God is : (1) to use any of these which can subserve the higher ends, (2) to purify such as have been misused, (3) to introduce new ideas and modes of looking at things, and (4) to combat what is wrong and cannot be mended : all for the purpose of leading to the truth and gradually letting in spiritual light where there was darkness before. If that is not done with discretion and the skill of a spiritual Teacher, there may be not only a reaction of obstinacy, but an unseemly show of dishonour to the true God and His Truth, and doubts would spread among the weaker brethren whose faith is shallow and infirm. What happens to individuals is true collectively of nations or groups of people. They think in their self-obsession that their own ideas are right God in His infinite compassion bears with them, and asks those who have purer ideas of faith not to vilify the weaknesses of their neighbours, lest the neighbours in their turn vilify the real truth and make matters even worse than before. In so far as there are mistakes, God will forgive and send His grace for helping ignorance and folly. In so far as there is active evil, He will deal with it in His own way. Of course the righteous man must not hide his light under a bushel, or compromise with evil, or refuse to establish right living where he has the power to do so.

Among you laugh at others :[113]
It may be that
The (latter) are better
Than the (former):
Nor let some women
Laugh at others :
It may be that
The (latter) are better
Than the (former):
Nor defame nor be[114]
Sarcastic to each other,
Nor call each other
By (offensive) nicknames :
Ill-seeming is a name
Connoting wickedness,
(To be used of one)
After he has believed :
And those who
Do not desist are
(Indeed) doing wrong.

113. Mutual ridicule ceases to be fun when there is arrogance or selfishness or malice behind it. We may laugh *with* people, to share in the happiness of life : we must never laugh *at* people in contempt or ridicule. In many things they may be better than ourselves !

114. Defamation may consist in speaking ill of others by the spoken or written word, or in acting in such a way as to suggest a charge against some person whom we are not in a position to judge. A cutting, biting remark or taunt or sarcasm is included in the word *lamaza*. An offensive nickname may amount to dafamation, but in any case there is no point in using offensive nicknames, or names that suggest some real or fancied defect. They ill accord with the serious purpose which Muslims should have in life. For example, even if a man is lame it is wrong to address him as "O lame one!" It causes him pain and it is bad manners. So in the case of the rude remark "the black man".

SUSPICION

XLIX : 12

O Ye who believe !
Avoid suspicion as much [115]
(As possible) : for suspicion
In some cases is a sin :
And spy not on each other,
Nor speak ill of each other
Behind their backs. Would any
Of you like to eat
The flesh of his dead [116]
Brother ? Nay, ye would
Abhor it . . . But fear God :
For God is Oft-returning,
Most Merciful.

SETTING EQUALS TO GOD

IV : 48

God forgiveth not
That equals should be set up

115. Most kinds of suspicion are baseless and to be avoided, and some are crimes in themselves : for they do cruel injustice to innocent men and women. Spying, or enquiring too curiously into other people's affairs, means either idle curiosity and is therefore futile, or suspicion carried a stage further, which almost amounts to sin. Back-biting also is a brood of the same genus. It may be either futile but all the same mischievous, or it may be poisoned with malice, in which case it is a sin added to sin.

116. No one would like even to think of such an abomination as eating the flesh of his brother. But when the brother is dead and the flesh is carrion, abomination is added to abomination. In the same way we are asked to refrain from hurting people's feelings when they are present ; how much worse is it when we say things, true or false, when they are absent !

With Him; but He forgiveth
Anything else, to whom
He pleaseth ; to set up
Equals with God
Is to devise a sin [117]
Most heinous indeed.

VI : 151

Say : " Come I will rehearse
What God hath (really) [118]
Prohibited you from " : join not
Anything as equal with Him;

117. Just as in an earthly kingdom the worst crime is that of treason, as it cuts at the very existence of the State, so in the spiritual kingdom, the unforgivable sin is that of contumacious treason against God by putting up God's creatures in rivalry against Him. This is rebellion against the essence and source of spiritual Life. It is what Plato would call the " lie in the soul ". But even here, if the rebellion is through ignorance, and is followed by sincere repentance and amendment, God's mercy is always open.

118. Instead of following pagan superstitions, and being in constant terror of imaginary taboos and prohibitions, we should study the true moral law, whose sanction is God's Law. The first step is that we should recognize that He is the One and Only Lord and Cherisher. The mention of goodness to parents immediately afterwards suggests : (1) that God's love of us and care for us may—on an infinitely higher plane—be understood by our ideal of parental love, which is purely unselfish ; (2) that our first duty among our fellow creatures is to our father and mother, whose love leads us to the conception of divine love. Arising from that is the conception of our converse duties to our children. God provides sustenance (material and spiritual) not only for us, but for them ; hence any custom like the pagan custom of sacrificing children to Moloch stands condemned. Then come the moral prohibitions against lewdness and all unseemly acts, relating to sex or otherwise, open or secret. This is followed by the prohibition of killing or fighting. All these things are comformable to our own interests, and therefore true wisdom from our own point of view.

Be good to your parents ;
Kill not your children
On a plea of want ;—We
Provide sustenance for you
And for them ;—come not
Nigh to shameful deeds,
Whether open or secret ;
Take not life, which God
Hath made sacred, except
By way of justice and law : [119]
Thus doth He command you,
That ye may learn wisdom.

SHAMEFUL DEEDS

VII : 33

Say : The things that my Lord
Hath indeed forbidden are : [120]

119. For the comprehensive word *haqq* I have used the two words "justice and law" : other significations implied are : right, truth, what is becoming, etc. It is not only that human life is sacred, but all life is sacred. Even in killing animals for food, a dedicatory formula "in the name of God" has to be employed, to make it lawful.

120. The forbidden things are described in four categories : (1) what is shameful or unbecoming ; the sort of things which have also legal and social sanctions, not of a local but of a universal kind ; that may be called offences against society; (2) sins against self and trespasses or excesses of every sort ; these are against truth and reason ; here would come in indiscipline, failure in doing intangible duties not clearly defined by law ; selfishness or self-aggrandisement, which may be condoned by custom and not punished by law, etc.; (3) erecting fetishes or false gods, this is treason against the true God ; and (4) corrupting religion by debasing superstitions, etc.

Shameful deeds, whether open
Or secret ; sins and trespasses
Against truth or reason ; assigning
Of partners to God, for which
Ye are given no authority ;
And saying things about God
Of which ye have no knowledge.

SLANDER

IV : 148

God loveth not that evil
Should be noised abroad [121]
In public speech, except
Where injustice hath been
Done ; for God
Is He who heareth
And knoweth all things.

121. We can make a public scandal of evil in many ways. (1) It may be idle sensation-mongering : it often leads to more evil by imitation, as where criminal deeds are glorified in a cinema or talked about shamelessly in a novel or drama. (2) It may be malicious gossip of a personal kind : it does no good, but it hurts people's feelings. (3) It may be malevolent slander or libel : it is intended deliberately to cause harm to people's reputation or injure them in other ways, and is rightly punishable under all laws. (4) It may be a public rebuke or correction or remonstrance, without malice. (1), (2) and (3) are absolutely forbidden. (4) may be by a person in authority ; in which case the exception applies, for all wrong or injustice must be corrected openly, to prevent its recurrence. Or (4) may be by a person not vested with authority, but acting either from motives of public spirit or in order to help some one who has been wronged ; here again the exception will apply. But if the motive is different, the exception does not apply. (4) Would also include a public complaint by a person who has suffered a wrong ; he has every right to seek public redress.

THROWING FAULT ON INNOCENT

IV : 112

But if any one earns
A fault or a sin
And throws it on to one
That is innocent,
He carries (on himself)
(Both) a falsehood
And a flagrant sin.

USURY

II : 275

Those who devour usury [122]
Will not stand except

122. Usury is condemned and prohibited in the strongest possible terms. There can be no question about the prohibition. When we come to the definition of Usury, there is room for difference of opinion. Hadhrat Umar, according to Ibn Kathir, felt some difficulty in the matter, as the Apostle left this world before the details of the question were settled. This was one of the three questions on which he wished he had had more light from the Apostle, the other two being Khilafat and Kalalat. Our Ulama, ancient and modern, have worked out a great body of literature on Usury, based mainly on economic conditions as they existed at the rise of Islam. I agree with them on the main principles but respectfully differ from them on the definition of Usury. As this subject is highly controversial, I shall discuss it, not in this Commentary but on a suitable occasion elsewhere. The definition I would accept would be : undue profit made, not in the way of legitimate trade, out of loans of gold and silver, and necessary articles of food, such as wheat, barley, dates, and salt (according to the list mentioned by the holy apostle himself). My definition would include profiteering of all kinds, but exclude economic credit, the creature of modern banking and finance.

As stands one whom
The Evil One by his touch
Hath driven to madness [123]
That is because they say :
" Trade is like usury ". [124]
But God hath permitted trade
And forbidden usury.
Those who after receiving
Direction from their Lord,
Desist, shall be pardoned
For the past ; their case
Is for God (to judge) ;
But those who repeat
(The offence) are Companions
Of the Fire : they will
Abide therein (for ever).

II : 278 to 280

278. O ye who believe !
Fear God, and give up
What remains of your demand
For Usury, if ye are
Indeed believers.

123. An apt simile : whereas legitimate trade or industry increases the prosperity and stability of men and nations, a dependence on Usury would merely encourage a race of idlers, cruel blood-suckers, and worthless fellows who do not know their own good and are therefore akin to madmen.

124. The sharp opposition between legitimate trade and usury supports my definition in the last note but one. *Bai* (literally sale or barter) is also used more generally for trade and commerce and various kinds of transactions.

279. If ye do it not,
Take notice of war[125]
From God and His Apostle :
But if ye turn back,
Ye shall have
Your capital sums :
Deal not unjustly
And ye shall not
Be dealt with unjustly.
280. If the debtor is
In a difficulty,
Grant him time
Till it is easy
For him to repay.
But if ye remit it
By way of charity,
That is best for you
If ye only knew.

WASTING

VI : 141

It is He who produceth
Gardens, with trellises
And without, and dates,
And tilth with produce
Of all kinds, and olives
And pomegranates,
Similar (in kind)
And different (in variety) :

125. This is not war for opinions, but an ultimatum of war for the liberation of debtors unjustly dealt with and oppressed.

Eat of their fruit
In their season, but render
The dues that are proper
On the day that the harvest
Is gathered. But waste not[126]
By excess : for God
Loveth not the wasters.

VII : 31

O Children of Adam !
Wear your beautiful apparel[127]
At every time and place
Of prayer : eat and drink :
But waste not by excess,
For God loveth not the wasters.

126. "Waste not, want not," says the English proverb. Here the same wisdom is preached from a higher motive See what magnificent means God provides in nature for the sustenance of all His creatures, because He loves them all Enjoy them in moderation and be grateful. But commit no excess, and commit no waste : the two things are the same from different angles of vision. If you do, you take away something from other creatures and God would not like your selfishness.

127. *Beautiful apparel : Zinat* adornments or apparel for beautiful living : construed to mean not only clothes that add grace to the wearer, but toilet and cleanliness, attention to hair, and other small personal details which no self-respecting man or woman ought to neglect when going solemnly even before a great human dignitary, if only out of respect for the dignity of the occasion. How much more important it is to attend to these details when we solemnly apply our minds to the Presence of God, though He is always present everywhere ! But the caution against excess applies : men must not go to prayer in silks or ornaments, appropriate to women. Similarly sober food, good and wholesome is not to be divorced from offices of religion ; only the caution against excess applies strictly. A dirty, unkempt, slovenly Faqir could not claim sanctity in Islam.

WORSHIPPING OTHERS THAN GOD

II : 165

Yet there are men
Who take (for worship)
Others besides God,
As equal (with God):
They love them
As they should love God.
But those of Faith are
Overflowing in their love
For God.
If only the unrighteous
Could see, they would see
The Penalty: that to God
Belongs all power, and God
Will strongly enforce
The Penalty.[128]

128. Everything around and within us points to unity of purpose and design,—points to God. Yet there are foolish persons (unrighteous = those who deliberately use the choice given them to go wrong). They think something else is equal to God. Perhaps they even do lip service to God, but their heart is in their fetish,—unlike the heart of the righteous, who are wholly devoted and absorbed in the love of God. If only the unrighteous could see the consequences, they would see the terrible Penalty, and that all Power is in God's hands, not in that of any one else. Who are these others who are used as fetishes by the misguided? It may be: (1) Creatures of their own imagination, or of their faculties misused; the idea lying behind idols is akin to this, for no intelligent idol-worshipper owns to worshipping stocks and stones; or (2) good leaders whose names have been misused out of perversity to erect them to a position of equality with God; or (3) Powers of evil that deliberately mislead. When it comes to the inevitable consequences of blasphemy and the rejection of God, the eyes of all are opened and these false and artificial relations dissolve. The idea which was created into a fetish disowns its follower, *i.e.*, is seen to have no reasonable basis in the life of the follower, and

WINE AND GAMBLING

II : 219

They ask thee
Concerning wine [129] and gambling.[130]
Say : " In them is great sin,
And some profit, for men;
But the sin is greater
Than the profit."

the follower is forced to renounce it as false. The good leaders whose names were misused would of course disown the misuse of their names, and the evil ones would take an unholy delight in exposing the facts. The Reality is now irresistible but alas ! at what cost ?

129. *Wine : Khamr* : literally understood to mean the fermented juice of the grape; applied by analogy to all fermented liquor, and by further analogy to any intoxicating liquor or drug. There may possibly be some benefit in it, but the harm is greater than the benefit, especially if we look at it from a social as well as an individual point of view.

130 *Gambling : Maisir* : literally, a means of getting something too easily, getting a profit without working for it ; hence gambling. That is the principle on which gambling is prohibited. The form most familiar to the Arabs was gambling by casting lots by means of arrows, on the principle of a lottery : the arrows were marked, and served the same purpose as a modern lottery ticket. Something, *e.g.*, the carcase of a slaughtered animal, was divided into unequal parts. The marked arrows were drawn from a bag. Some were blank and those who drew them got nothing. Others indicated prizes, which were big or small. Whether you got a big share or a small share, or nothing, depended on pure luck, unless there was fraud also on the part of some persons concerned. The principle on which the objection is based is: that, even if there is no fraud, you gained what you have not earned, or lose on a mere chance. Dice and wagering are rightly held to be within the definition of gambling. But insurance is not gambling, when conducted on business principles. Here the basis for calculation is statistics on a large scale, from which mere chance is eliminated. The insurers themselves pay premia in proportion to risks, exactly and statistically calculated.

They ask thee how much
They are to spend;
Say: "What is beyond [131]
Your needs."
Thus doth God
Make clear to you
His Signs: in order that
Ye may consider.

---

131. Hoarding is no use either to ourselves, or to any one else. We should use the wealth we need; any superfluities we must spend in good works or in charity.

III.—BELIEFS OF ISLAM

BAPTISM OF GOD

II : 138

(Our religion is)
The Baptism of God: [132]
And who can baptize better
Than God ? And it is He
Whom we worship.

BURDEN OF SIN

LIII : 38 and 39

38. That no bearer of burden (of sins)
Can bear the burden of another ;
39. And that man shall have nothing
But what he strives for.

132. *Sibgat* : baptism : the root meaning implies a dye o colour ; apparently the Arab Christians mixed a dye or colou in the baptismal water, signifying that the baptized perso got a new colour in life. We do not believe that it i necessary to be baptized to be saved. Our higher baptisr is the "Baptism" of God, by which we take on a colou (symbolically) of God, and absorb His goodness in us.

The accusative case of *Sibgat* puts it in apposition to *Milla* (" religion ").

BELIEVERS WILL BE TESTED

XXIX : 2

Do men think that
They will be left alone
On Saying, "We believe",[133]
And that they will not
Be tested?

BELIEVE IN GOD AND ACT RIGHTEOUSLY

II : 62

Those who believe (in the Quran),
And those who follow the Jewish
(scriptures),
And the Christians and the Sabians,—[134]
Any who believe in God,

133. Mere lip profession of Faith is not enough. It must be tried and tested in the real turmoil of life. The test will be applied in all kinds of circumstances, in individual life and in relation to the environment around us, to see whether we can strive constantly and put God above Self. Much pain, sorrow, and self-sacrifice may be necessary, not because they are good in themselves, but because they will purify us, like fire applied to a goldsmith's crucible to burn out the dross.

134. Latest researches have revealed a small remnant of a religious community numbering about 2,000 souls in lower Iraq near Basra. In Arabic they are called *Subbi* (plural, *Subba*). They are also called Sabians and Nasoræans or Mandæans or Christians of St. John. They claim to be Gnostics or knowers of the Great Life. They dress in white, and believe in frequent immersions in water. Their book Ginza is in a dialect of

And the Last Day,
And work righteousness,
Shall have their reward
With their Lord : on them
Shall be no fear, nor shall they grieve.[135]

Aramaic. They have theories of Darkness and Light as in Zoroastrianism. They use the name *Yardan* (Jordan) for any river. They live in peace and harmony among their Muslim neighbours. They resemble the Sabi-un mentioned in the Quran, but are not probably identical with them.

The pseudo-Sabians of Harran, who attracted the attention of Khalifa Mamun-al-Rashid in 830 A.D. by their long hair and peculiar dress probably adopted the name as it was mentioned in the Quran, in order to claim the privileges of the People of the Book. They were Syrian Star-Worshippers with Hellenistic tendencies, like the Jews contemporary with Jesus. It is doubtful whether they had any right to be called People of the Book in the technical sense of the term. But I think that in this matter the term can be extended by analogy to cover earnest followers of Zoroaster, the Vedas, Buddha, Confucius and other teachers of the Moral Law.

There was another people called the Sabæans, who played an important part in the histoty of early Arabia and are known through their inscriptions in an alphabet allied to the Phœnician and the Babylonian. They had a flourishing kingdom in the Yemen tract in South Arabia about 800-700 B.C., though their origin may have been in North Arabia. They worshipped the planets and Stars (Moon, Sun, Venus). Probably the queen of Sheba is connected with them. They succumbed to Abyssinia about 350 A.D. and to Persia about 579 A.D. Their capital was near Sanaa. They had beautiful stone buildings, in which the pointed arch is noticeable.

135. The point of the verse is that Islam does not teach an exclusive doctrine, and is not meant exclusively for one people. The Jews claimed this for themselves, and the Christians in their origin were a sect of the Jews. Even the modern organized Christian Churches, though they have been, consciously or unconsciously, influenced by the Time-spirit, including the historical fact of Islam, yet cling to the idea of Vicarious Atonement, which means that all who do not believe in it or who lived previously to the death of Christ are at a disadvantage spiritually before the Throne of God. The attitude of Islam is entirely different. Islam existed before the preaching of Muhammad on this earth : the Quran expressly calls Abraham a Muslim.

II : 186

When My servants
Ask thee concerning Me,
I am indeed
Close (to them) : I listen
To the prayer of every
Suppliant when he calleth on Me :
Let them also, with a will,
Listen to My call,
And believe in Me :
That they may walk
In the right way.[136]

IV : 122 and 123

122. But those who believe
And do deeds of righteousness,—
We shall soon admit them
To Gardens, with rivers
Flowing beneath,—to dwell
Therein for ever.
God's promise is the truth,
And whose word can be
Truer than God's ?
123. Not your desires, nor those [137]
Of the People of the Book

Its teaching (submission to God's will) has been and will be the teaching of Religion for all time and for all peoples.

136. This verse 186 is not foreign to the subject of Ramadhan, but emphasize its spiritual aspect. Here we are told of Prayer and the nearness of God, and we are asked not to "eat up" other people's substance.

137. Personal responsibility is again and again insisted on as

(Can prevail) : whoever
Works evil, will be
Requited accordingly.
Nor will he find, besides God,
Any protector or helper.

V : 72

Those who believe (in the Quran),
Those who follow the Jewish (scriptures),
And the Sabians and the Christians,—
Any who believe in God
And the Last Day,
And work righteousness,— [138]
On them shall be no fear,
Nor shall they grieve.

XVIII : 88

" But whoever believes,
And works righteousness,—
He shall have a goodly
Reward, and easy will be

the key-note of Islam. In this are implied faith and right conduct. Faith is not an external thing : it begins with an act of will, but if true and sincere, it affects the whole being, and leads to right conduct. In this it is distinguished from the kind of faith which promises salvation because some one else in whom you are asked to believe has borne away the sins of men, or the kind of faith which says that because you are born of a certain race ("Children of Abraham") or a certain caste, you are privileged, and your conduct will be judged by a different standard from that of other men. Whatever you are, if you do evil, you must suffer the consequences, unless God's Mercy comes to your help.

138. As God's Message is one, Islam recognizes true faith in other forms, provided that it be sincere, supported by reason, and backed up by righteous conduct.

His task as we order it
By our command." [139]
God has promised, to those
Among you who believe.

XXIV : 55 (part)

And work righteous deeds, that He [140]
Will, of a surety, grant them
In the land, inheritance
(Of power), as He granted it
To those before them ; that
He will establish in authority
Their religion—the one
Which He has chosen for them ;
And that He will change
(Their state), after the fear [141]

139. He never said like Pharaoh, "I am your Lord Most High!" On the contrary his punishments were humbly regulated as not being final, and he laid more stress on the good he could do to those who lived normal lives in faith and righteousness. His rule was easy to them : he imposed no heavy tasks because of his power, but gave every opportunity to rich and poor for the exercise of virtue and goodness. Such is the spiritual lesson to be learned from the first episode.

140. Three things are promised here, to those who have Faith and obey God's Law : (1) that they will inherit power and authority in the land, not for any selfish purposes of theirs nor by way of favouritism, but in order that they may maintain God's Law ; (2) that the Religion of Right, which God has chosen for them, will be openly established, and will suppress all wrong and oppression ; (3) that the righteous will live in peace and security, instead of having to suffer persecution, or leave their hearths and homes for the cause of God, or practise the rites of their Faith in secret.

141. If this verse was revealed about the time of the Battle of the Ditch (*Khandaq*), also called the Battle of the Confederates (*Ahzab*), A.H. 4-5, we can imagine the comfort it gave to the Muslims who were besieged in Medina by a force ten times their number. The Muslims then lived in a state of great

In which they (lived), to one
Of security and peace :
" They will worship Me (alone)
And not associate aught with Me."
If any do reject Faith
After this, they are
Rebellious and wicked.

FOLLOW GOD's GUIDANCE

XX : 123 (part) and 124

123. Whosoever
Follows My guidance, will not
Lose his way, nor fall [142]
Into misery.
124. " But whosoever turns away
From My Message, verily
For him is a life narrowed
Down, and We shall raise
Him up blind on the Day [143]
Of Judgment."

suspense and danger, and under arms for days on end. The security and authority they were promised came to them subsequently in abundant measure.

142. We have here the consequences of Guidance to the individual, *viz.*: being saved from going astray or from falling into misery and despair. The consequences, expressed, though they apply to the individual, are also appropriate taken collectively : " on them shall be no fear, nor shall they grieve."

143. The consequences of the rejection of God's guidance are here expressed more individually : a life narrowed down, and a blindness that will persist beyond this life. " A life narrowed

II : 206

When it is said to him :
" Fear God,"
He is led by arrogance
To (more) crime.
Enough for him is Hell;—
What a bed of misery! [144]

FEAR NONE EXCEPT GOD

IX : 18

The mosques of God
Shall be visited and maintained
By such as believe in God
And the Last Day, establish
Regular prayers, and practise
Regular charity, and fear
None (at all) except God.[145]
It is they who are expected
To be on true guidance.[146]

down," has many implications: (1) it is a life from which all the beneficent influences of God's wide world are excluded; (2) it is a life for Self, not for all; (3) in looking exclusively to the "good things" of this life, it misses the true Reality.

144. According to the English saying, "As you have made your bed, so you must lie in it."

145. Sincere Believers are those who have faith in God and the future, and have a spirit of devotion and charity—a true and abiding spirit, not merely isolated acts now and again. Moreover they must not bow to worldly greed or ambition which produces fear of worldly power.

146. Others may call themselves by what names they like. True guidance is shown by the tests here indicated.

LVII : 28

O ye that believe![147]
Fear God, and believe
In His Apostle, and He will
Bestow on you a double[148]
Portion of His Mercy
He will provide for you
A Light by which ye[149]
Shall walk (straight
In your path), and He
Will forgive you (your past:)[150]

147. From the context before and after this is held to refer to the Christians and People of the Book who kept their Faith true and undefiled.

148 The double portion refers to the past and the future. As noted in the last note, this passage is addressed to the Christians and the People of the Book, who, when honestly facing the question of the new Revelation in Islam, find in it the fulfilment of previous revelations, and therefore believe in God's Apostle Muhammad, and walk by the new Light. Their previous merits will be duly recognized, and they will be treated on fully equal terms in the new Ummat. This is their double share, not necessarily more in quantity than that of their brethren in Islam who passed through no other gate, but having a twofold aspect.

149. As this refers to the Christians and the People of the Book, the following saying of Christ in his last days may interest them: "'Yet a little while is the light with you. Walk while ye have the light, lest darkness come upon you ...... While ye have the light, believe in the light, that ye may be the children of light.' These things spake Jesus, and departed, and did hide himself from them." (John, xii. 35-36.) The light of Christ's Gospel soon departed; his Church was enveloped in darkness; then came the light again, in the fuller light of Islam. And they are asked to believe in the Light, and to walk in it.

150. Any wrongs they may have committed through ignorance or misconceptions in their previous religion will be forgiven them, as they have seen the new Light and walk by it.

For God is Oft-forgiving,
Most Merciful.

GOD'S MERCY

VII : 156 and 157 (parts)

156. He said : " With My Punishment
I visit whom I will ;
But My Mercy extendeth [151]
To all things. That (Mercy)
I shall ordain for those
Who do right, practise
Regular charity, and believe
in Our Signs ;—[152]
157. Those who follow the Apostle
The unlettered Prophet.

XII : 87

" O my sons ! go ye
And enquire about Joseph

151. God's mercy is in and for all things. All nature subserves a common purpose, which is for the good of all His creatures. Our faculties and our understandings are all instances of His grace and mercy. Each unit or factor among His creatures benefits from the others and receives them as God's Mercy to itself ; and in its turn, each contributes to the benefit of the others and is thus an instance of God's mercy to them. His mercy is universal and all pervasive ; while His justice and punishment are reserved for those who swerve from His plan and (to use a mediæval juridical formula) go out of His Peace.

152. The personal grace and mercy—and their opposite—are referred to the singular pronoun 'I' while the impersonal Law by which God's Signs operate in His universe, is referred to the plural pronoun of authority and dignity, " We "

And his brother, and never
Give up hope of God's
Soothing Mercy : [153] truly
No one despairs of God's
Soothing Mercy, except
Those who have no faith." [154]

GOD'S NAME INSPIRES AWE

VIII : 2

For, Believers are those
Who, when God is mentioned,
Feel a tremor in their hearts,
And when they hear
His Signs rehearsed, find
Their faith strengthened,
And put (all) their trust
In their Lord.

XXII : 34 (part) and 35

34. But your God is One God :
Submit then your wills to Him

153. The word is *rauh*, not *ruh*, as some translators have mistakenly construed it. *Rauh* includes the idea of a Mercy that stills or calms our distracted state, and is particularly appropriate here in the mouth of Jacob.

154. Jacob ignores and forgives the sting and malice in the speech of his sons, and like a true man of God, still wishes them well, gives them sound advice, and sends them on an errand which is to open their eyes to the wonderful ways of Providence as much as it will bring consolation to his own distressed soul. He asks them to go again in search of Joseph and Benjamin. Perhaps by now he had an idea that they might be together

(In Islam): and give thou
The good news [155] to those
Who humble themselves,—
35. To those whose hearts,
When God is mentioned,
Are filled with fear,
Who show patient perseverance
Over their afflictions, keep up
Regular prayer, and spend
(In charity) out of what
We have bestowed upon them.[156]

XVII : 56 and 57

56. Say : "Call on those—
Besides Him—whom ye fancy :
They have neither the power
To remove your troubles
From you nor toc hange them" [157]

in Egypt. In any case their stock of grain is again low, and they must seek its replenishment in Egypt.

155. *The good news : i e.*, the Message of God, that He will accept in us the sacrifice of self for the benefit of our fellow-men.

156. Some qualities of God's devotees are mentioned here, in ascending order: (1) Humility before God makes them receptive, and prepares them to listen to God's Message ; (2) fear of God, which is akin to love, touches their heart, and penetrates through their inmost being; (3) they are not afraid of anything in mortal life; they take their trials patiently, and they go on in a course of righteousness with constancy ; (4) their prayer now is not a matter of form, but a real communion with God, with a sense of confidence such as a faithful servant feels in the presence of a kind and loving master ; and (5) gratitude to God, as shown by practical acts of charity to all fellow-creatures.

157. Men's suspicions of each other or of the prophets have been condemned in the previous verses. We now have the strongest condemnation of all, that of imagining any other

57. Those whom they call upon
Do desire (for themselves) means
Of access to their Lord,—
Even those who are nearest :[158]
They hope for His Mercy
And fear His Wrath :
For the Wrath of thy Lord
Is something to take heed of.

GOD'S GRACIOUSNESS TO ALL ALIKE

XXIII : 88 to 90

88. Say : "Who is it in whose
Hands is the governance
Of all things,—who protects
(All), but is not protected
(Of any) ? (Say) if ye know."
89. They will say, "(It belongs)
To God." Say : "Then how
Are ye deluded ?"[159]

being as being equal or in the same category with the One Tru God. God has all power : they have no power. They cannc remove men's troubles. They cannot even mitigate or chang them so as to afford the least relief. Why indulge in fals worship ?

158. Where men or heroes, or prophets or angels a worshipped, the worship is futile; because (1) even if they a good and holy, and ever so near to God, yet the nearest of the have need to seek means of access to God, and they do see such means, *viz.*: the hope of God's Grace ; (2) though by the very nature it is impossible for us to suppose that they wi incur the Wrath of God, yet they are but creatures and a subject to the law of personal responsibility.

159. 'The order and unity of purpose in the Universe argu Unity of design and goodness in its Maker. Is it not then she madness for you to run after false fancies and fail to understar and obey His Will ? It is delusion in you to seek other than Goc

90. We have sent them the **Truth**:
But they indeed practise **Falsehood**!

GOD KEEPS IN CHECK ONE SET OF PEOPLE BY ANOTHER

II. 251 (part)

And did not God
Check one set of people
By means of another,
The earth would indeed
Be full of mischief:
But God is full of bounty
To all the worlds.[160]

GOOD PROCEEDS FROM GOD

IV : 79

Whatever good, (O man!)
Happens to thee, is from God;
But whatever evil happens
To thee, is from thy (own) soul.
And We have sent an Apostle[161]
To (instruct) mankind.

160. God's plan is universal. He loves and protects *all* His creatures and His bounties are for all worlds. To protect one He may have to check another but we must never lose faith that His love is for all in boundless measures.

161. To blame a man of God for our misfortunes is doubly unjust. For he comes to save us from misfortune, and it is because we flout him or pay no heed to him, that our own rebellion brings its own punishment. If we realize this truth

And enough is God
For a witness.

HUMILITY AND REMEMBERANCE

LVII : 16

Has not the time arrived[162]
For the Believers that
Their hearts in all humility
Should engage in the remembrance
Of God and of the Truth
Which has been revealed (to them),
And that they should not
Become like those to whom
Was given Revelation aforetime,[163]
But long ages passed over them

we shall be saved from two sins : (1) the sin of injustice to God's Messengers, who come for our good, and not for our harm ; and (2) the sin of not realizing our own shortcomings or rebellion, and thus living in spiritual darkness. If the Message is from God, that carries its own authority : "enough is God for a witness."

162. Humility and the remembrance of God and His Message are never more necessary than in the hour of victory and prosperity.

163. The men immediately referred to are the contemporary Jews and Christians To each of these Ummats was given God's Revelation, but as time passed, they corrupted it, became arrogant and hard hearted. and subverted justice, truth, and the purity of Life. But the general lesson is far wider. No one is favoured of God except on the score of righteousness Except on that score, there is no chosen individual or race. There is no blind good fortune or ill fortune. All happens according to the just laws and will of God. But at no time is humility or righteousness more necessary than in the hour of victory or triumph.

And their hearts grew hard ?
For many among them
Are rebellious transgressors.

INVOKE GOD ABOVE

XXXV : 13 (end) and 14

13. And those whom ye invoke
Besides Him have not
The least power.[164]

14. If ye invoke them,
They will not listen
To your call, and if [165]
They were to listen,
They cannot answer
Your (Prayer). On the Day
Of Judgment they will reject [166]
Your "Partnership". And none,

164. *Qitmir* : the thin, white skin that covers the date stone It has neither strength nor texture, and has no value whatever Anyone relying on any power other than that of God relies on nothing whatever. The *Qitmir* is worse than the proverbial "broken reed" At another place in the Holy Quran the word *naqir*, "the groove in a date stone", is used similarly for a thing of no value or significance.

165. False or imaginary objects of worship serve no purpose whatever. They cannot hear ; if they could hear, they could not grant prayers or petitions. In fact, if they are real creatures, such as angels, or deified human beings, they will very rightly, repudiate any such worship as brings them into competition or "partnership" with God. See next note.

166. No false ideas or false impressions will remain when true values are restored. Why not then accept the Truth now in this life, and get on to the true path of Grace ?

(O man!) can tell thee[167]
(The Truth) like the One
Who is acquainted with all things.

INVITATION TO PEOPLE OF THE BOOK

III : 64

Say: "O People
Of the Book! come
To common terms
As between us and you:
That we worship
None but God;
That we associate
No equals with Him;
That we erect, not,
From among ourselves,
Lords and patrons
Other than God."[168]
If then they turn back,
Say ye: "Bear witness
That we (at least)
Are Muslims (bowing
To God's will)."

167. None can tell you the Truth better than He Who is All-wise and All-knowing. Why not accept His Message and receive His guidance?

168. In the abstract the People of the Book would agree to all three propositions. In practice they fail. Apart from doctrinal lapses from the unity of the One True God, there is the question of a consecrated Priesthood (among the Jews it was hereditary also), as if a mere human being,—Cohen, or Pope, or Priest, or Brahman,—could claim superiority apart from his

XIII : 11 (part)

Verily never
Will God change the condition
Of a people until they
Change it themselves
(With their own souls).[169]

III : 31

Say : " If ye do love God,
Follow me : God will love you
And forgive you your sins :
For God is Oft-forgiving,
Most Merciful."

learning and the purity of his life or could stand between man and God in some special sense. The same remarks apply to the worship of saints. They may be pure and holy, but no one can protect us or claim Lordship over us except God. Abraham was a true man of God, but he could not be called a Jew or a Christian as he lived long before the Law of Moses or the Gospel of Jesus was revealed.

169. God is not intent on punishment. He created man virtuous and pure ; He gave him intelligence and knowledge ; He surrounded him with all sorts of instruments of His grace and mercy. If, in spite of all this, man distorts his own will and goes against God's Will, yet is God's forgiveness open to him if he will take it. It is only when he has made his own sight blind and changed his own nature or soul away from the beautiful mould in which God formed it, that God's Wrath will descend on him and the favourable position in which God placed him will be changed. When once the punishment comes, there is no turning it back. None of the things which he relied upon—other than God—can possibly protect him.

MOST RIGHTEOUS IS MOST HONOURED

XLIX : 13

O Mankind! We created [170]
You from a single (pair)
Of a male and a female,
And made you into
Nations and tribes, that
Ye may know each other
(Not that ye may despise
Each other). Verily
The most honoured of you
In the sight of God
Is (he who is) the most
Righteous of you.
And God has full knowledge
And is well acquainted
(With all things).

MISFORTUNE HAPPENS UNDER SOME RECORDED LAWS OF GOD

LVII : 22 to 24

22. No misfortune can happen
On earth or in your souls [171]

170. This is addressed to all mankind and not only to the Muslim brotherhood, though it is understood that in a perfected world the two would be synonymous. As it is, mankind is descended from one pair of parents. Their tribes, races, and nations are convenient labels by which we may know certain differing characteristics. Before God they are all one, and he gets most honour who is most righteous.

171. External disasters or misfortunes may strike people's eye or imagination, but there are worse crises and misfortunes in the spiritual world, which are of equal or greater importance

But is recorded in
A decree before We bring
It into existence:
That is truly easy for God:
In order that ye may
Not despair over matters
That pass you by,
Nor exult over favours
Bestowed upon you.
For God loveth not
Any vainglorious boaster,—[172]
Such persons as are[173]
Covetous and commend
Covetousness to men.
And if any turn back
(From God's Way), verily
God is free of all needs,
Worthy of all praise.

XLII : 30

Whatever misfortune
Happens to you, is because

to man's future. All this happens according to the Will and Plan of God. Even where we are allowed the exercise of our own wills, the consequences that follow are in accordance with the laws and Plan decreed by God beforehand.

172. In the external world, what people may consider misfortune or good fortune may both turn out to be illusory,—in Kipling's words, "both impostors just the same." The man of God does not grumble if some one else has possessions, nor exult if he has them. He does not covet and he does not boast. If he has any advantages, he shares them with other people, as he considers them not due to his own merits, but as gifts of God.

173. Neither the covetous nor the Boasters have any place in the Good Pleasure of God. The covetous are particularly

Of the things your hands [174]
Have wrought, and for many
(Of them) He grants forgiveness.

THY ALL FOR GOD

VI : 162

Say : " Truly, my prayer
And my service of sacrifice,
My lifé and my death,
Are (all) for God,
The Cherisher of the Worlds.

NO CHANGE IN WORDS OF GOD

X : 64 (part)

No change can there be
In the words of God [175]

insidious, as their avarice and niggardliness not only keep back the gifts of God from men, but their pernicious example dries up the streams of Charity in others.

174. All evil, all sorrow, all pain, and affliction, are things not normal, things twisted from the pure and holy nature as created by God's hands. As far as man is concerned, his misfortunes are but the consequences of the things he has done. He must bear personal responsibility for them and not throw the blame on others.

175. The Law of God is no respector of persons or races. In the words of Iqbal "Heaven favours neither you nor me." Every one is responsible for one's own doings and gets what one strives for.

XXXIII : 62 (part)

No change wilt thou find
In the practice (approved)
Of God.

NO ONE CAN HELP BUT GOD

III : 160

If God helps you,
None can overcome you:
If He forsakes you,
Who is there, after that,
That can help you?
In God, then,
Let Believers put their trust.

OBEY GOD

III : 132

And obey God
And the Apostle;
That ye may obtain mercy.

IV : 59

O ye who believe!
Obey God, and obey the Apostle
And those charged
With authority among you.[176]

176. *Ulu-l-amr*=those charged with authority or responsibility or decision, or the settlement of affairs. All ultimate authority rests in God. Men of God derive their authority

If ye differ in anything
Among yourselves, refer it
To God and His Apostle,
If ye do believe in God
And the Last Day:
That is best, and most suitable
For final determination.

IV : 69

All who obey God
And the Apostle
Are in the company
Of those on whom
Is the Grace of God,—
Of the Prophets (who teach),
The Sincere (lovers of Truth),
The Witnesses (who testify),
And the Righteous (who do good):
Ah ! what a beautiful Fellowship ! [177]

from Him. As Islam makes no sharp division between sacred and secular affairs, it expects ordinary governments to be imbued with righteousness, and stand in the place of the righteous Imam, and we must respect and obey such authority; otherwise there will be no order or discipline. Where, in actual fact, there is a sharp division between law and morality, between secular and religious affairs, as is the case in most countries at the present day, Islam still expects secular authority to be exercised in righteousness, and on that condition, enjoins obedience to such authority.

177. A passage of the deepest spiritual meaning. Even the humblest man who accepts Faith and does good becomes at once an accepted member of a great and beautiful spiritual Fellowship. It is a company which lives perpetually in the sunshine of God's Grace. It is a glorious hierachy, of which four grades are specified : (1) The highest is that of the Prophets or Apostles, who get plenary inspiration from God, and who teach mankind by example and precept. That rank in Islam is held

IV : 80

He who obeys
The Apostle, obeys God :
But if any turn away,
We have not sent thee
To watch over
(Their evil deeds).[178]

NO RESTRICTION AS TO PLACE OF WORSHIP

II : 114

And who is more unjust
Than he who forbids[179]

by Mohammad Mustafa. (2) the next are those whose badge is sincerity and truth ; they love and support the truth with their person, their means, their influence, and all that is theirs. That rank was held by the special Companions of Mohammad, among whom the type was that of Hadhrat Abu Bakr Siddiq. (3) the next are the noble army of Witnesses, who testify to the truth. The testimony may be by martyrdom, as in the case of Imams Hasan and Husain. Or it may be by the tongue of the true Preacher or the pen of the devoted scholar, or the life of the man devoted to service. (4) Lastly there is the large company of Righteous people, the ordinary folk who do their ordinary business, but always in a righteous way. They are the rank and file of the beautiful Fellowship, in which each has his place and yet all feel that they derive glory from the common association.

178. The Apostle was sent to preach, guide, instruct, and show the Way,—not to drive people to good, or to detect all that was evil. That is not God's Plan, which trains the human Will. The Apostle's duty is therefore to convey the Message of God, in all the ways of persuasion that are open to him. If men perversely disobey that Message, they are not disobeying him but they are disobeying God. In the same way those who obey the Message are obeying God. They are not obliging the Messenger : they are merely doing their duty.

179. There were actually Pagans in Mecca who tried to shut out the Muslim Arabs from the Kaaba, the universal place

That in places for the worship
Of God, God's name should be
Celebrated?—whose zeal
Is (in fact) to ruin them?
It was not fitting that such
Should themselves enter them
Except in fear. For them
There is nothing but disgrace
In this world, and in the world
To come, an exceeding torment.

NO COMPULSION IN RELIGION

II : 256

Let there be no compulsion [180]
In religion : Truth stands out

of Arab worship. The Pagans themselves called it the House o God. With what face could they exclude the Muslims, wh wanted to worship the true God instead of worshipping idols? If these Pagans had succeeded, they woul only have caused violent divisions among the Arabs an destroyed the sanctity and the very existence of the Kaba.

This verse, taken in a general sense, establishes the principl of freedom of worship in a public mosque or place dedicate to the orship of God. This is recognized in Muslim law There may be differences of opinion between one individua and another, or between one group and another as to th nature of God or the proper mode of worship, but no test can be laid down, nor can one individual or sect exclud another. So long as a person enters reverently and does nothin outwardly to cause offence to the other worshippers, he has right to go and worship in a public place set apart for God' worship.

180. Compulsion is incompatible with religion : because (1 religion depends upon faith and will, and these would be meaningless if induced by force ; (2) Truth and Error have been s clearly shown up by the mercy of God that there should be n doubt in the minds of any persons of good-will as to th

Clear from Error : whoever
Rejects Evil and believes
In God hath grasped
The most trustworthy
Hand-hold, that never breaks.
And God heareth
And knoweth all things.

PRAISE GOD

III : 190 and 191

190. Behold ! In the creation
Of the heavens and earth,
And the alternation
Of the Day and the Night,—[181]
There are indeed Signs
For men of understanding,—
191. Men who celebrate
The praises of God,
Standing, sitting,
And lying down on their sides [182]
And contemplate
The (wonders of) creation

fundamentals of faith ; (3) God's protection is continuous, and His plan is always to lead us from the depths of darkness into the clearest light.

181. The two items mentioned here are just brief symbols recalling the six or seven mentioned in the other passage. And those two are but brief symbols and reminders of the glorious majesty of God and His goodness to man.

182. That is, in all postures, which again is symbolical of all circumstances, personal, social, economic, historical, and other.

In the heavens and earth,
(With the thought):
"Our Lord! not for naught
Hast thou created (all) this!
Glory to Thee! Give us[183]
Salvation from the Penalty
Of the Fire.

PRINCIPLE OF RELIGIOUS TEACHING

XVI : 125

Invite (all) to the Way
Of thy Lord with wisdom
And beautiful preaching;
And argue with them
In ways that are best
And most gracious:[184]

183. It is the thought of Salvation that connects all these glories with man. Otherwise man would be a miserable, contemptible creature, in these beauties and wonders of Nature. With his high destiny of Salvation he can be lifted even higher than these glories! The fire is a symbol of penalty. We pray for salvation from the penalty.

184. In this wonderful passage are laid down principles of religious teaching which are good for all time But where are the Teachers with such qualifications? We must invite all to the Way of God, and expound His Universal Will; we must do it with wisdom and discretion, meeting people on their own ground and convincing them with illustrations from their own knowledge and experience. which may be very narrow, or very wide. Our preaching must be, not dogmatic. not self-regarding, not offensive. but gentle, considerate, and such as would attract their attention. Our manner and our arguments should not be acrimonious, but modelled on the most courteous and most gracious example, so that the hearer may say to himself, "This man is not dealing merely with dialectics; he is not trying to get a rise out of me; he is sincerely expounding the faith that is in him, and his motive is the love of man and the love of God".

For thy Lord knoweth best,
Who have strayed from His Path,
And who receive guidance.[185]

Qadha AND *Qadr*

VI : 125 (part)

Those whom God (in His Plan)
Willeth to guide,—He openeth [186]
Their breast to Islam.

REMEMBER GOD

VII : 205

And do thou (O reader !)
Bring thy Lord to remembrance

185. It may be that the Preacher sometimes says to himself "What is the use of teaching these people? They have made up their minds, or they are obstinate, or they are only trying to catch me out." Let him not yield to such a thought. Who knows how the seed of the Word of God may germinate in people's minds? It is not for man to look for results. Man's inner thoughts are known best to God.

186. God's Universal Plan is the *Qadha wa Qadr*, which is so much misunderstood. That Plan is unalterable, and that is His Will. It means that in the spiritual world, as in the physical world, there are laws of justice, mercy, grace, penalty, etc, which work as surely as anything we know. If, then, a man refuses Faith, becomes a rebel, with each step he goes further and further down, and his pace will be accellerated ; he will scarcely be able to take spiritual breath, and his recovery,—in spite of God's mercy which he has rejected,—will be as difficult as if he had to climb up to the skies. On the other hand, the godly will find, with each step, the next step easier. Jesus expressed this

In thy (very) soul,
With humility and in reverence,
Without loudness in words,
In the mornings and evenings;
And be not thou
Of those who are unheedful.

II : 152

Then do ye remember [187]
Me; I will remember
You. Be grateful to Me,
And reject not Faith.

truth paradoxically: "he that hath, to him shall be given; but he that hath not, from him shall be taken away even that which he hath": Mark iv, 25. John (vi. 65) makes Jesus say: "No man can come unto me, except it were given unto him of my Father"

187. The word "remember" is too pale a word for *Zikr*, which has now acquired a large number of associations in our religious literature, especially Sufi literature. In its verbal signification it implies: to remember; to praise by frequently mentioning; to rehearse; to celebrate or commemorate; to make much of; to cherish the memory of as a precious possession.

In Sufi devotions Zikr represents both a solemn ritual and a spiritual state of mind or heart, in which the devotee seeks to realize the presence of God. Thus there is Zikr of the mind and Zikr of the heart. For beginners the one may lead to the other; but in many cases the two may be simultaneous. There is a subtler distinction, between the Zikr that is open, and the Zikr that is secret, corresponding to the two doors of the heart, the fleshly and the spiritual. In English, some account (very imperfect) of Zikr will be found in Hughes's Dictionary of Islam, covering over 14 columns.

There is a great deal of mystic doctrine in this verse. That it is linked with the institution of the Qibla shows that the Qibla is itself connected with a great many root-ideas of the mystical interpretation of Unity.

IV : 1

O mankind ! reverence
Your Guardian-Lord,
Who created you
From a single Person,[188]
Created, of like nature,
His mate, and from them twain
Scattered (like seeds)
Countless men and women ;—
Reverence God, through Whom [189]
Ye demand your mutual (rights),
And (reverence) the wombs [190]
(That bore you) : for God
Ever watches over you.

188. *Nafs* may mean : (1) soul ; (2) self ; (3) person, living person ; (4) will, good pleasure. *Minha* : I follow the construction suggested by Imam Razi. The particle *min* would then suggest here not a portion or a source of something else, but a species, a nature, a similarity. The pronoun *ha* refers of course to *nafs*. The Biblical story of the creation of Eve from a rib of Adam may be allegorical, but we need not assume it in Quranic teaching.

189. All our mutual rights and duties are referred to God. We are His creatures ; His Will is the standard and measure of Good ; and our duties are measured by our conformity with His Will. "Our wills are ours, to make them Thine," says Tennyson (In Memoriam). Among ourselves (human beings) our mutual rights and duties arise out of God's Law, the sense of Right that is implanted in us by Him.

190. Among the most wonderful mysteries of our nature is that of sex. The unregenerate male is apt, in the pride of his physical strength, to forget the all-important part which the female plays in his very existence and in all the social relationships that arise in our collective human lives. The mother that bore us must ever have our reverence. The wife, through whom we enter parentage, must have our reverence. Sex , which governs so much of our physical life, and has so much influence on our emotional and higher nature, deserves - not our fear, or our contempt, or our amused indulgence, but—our reverence in the

XLII : 13

The same religion has He
Established for you as that
Which He enjoined on Noah—[191]
That which We have sent
By inspiration to thee—
And that which We enjoined
On Abraham, Moses, and Jesus :
Namely, that ye should remain
Steadfast in Religion, and make
No divisions therein : [192]
To those who worship
Other things than God,
Hard is the (way)
To which thou callest them [193]
God chooses to Himself those
Whom He pleases,
And guides to Himself
Those who turn (to Him).

highest sense of the term. With this fitting introduction we enter on a discussion of women, orphans, and family relationships.

191. God's Religion is the same in essence, whether given, for example, to Noah, Abraham, Moses, or Jesus, or to our holy Prophet. The source of unity is the revelation from God. In Islam it is "established" as an institution, and does not remain merely a vague suggestion.

192. Faith, Duty, or Religion, is not a matter to dispute about. The formation of sects is against the very principle of Religion and Unity. What we should strive for is steadfastness in duty and faith, and unity among mankind.

193. Unity, unselfishness, love for God and man,—these things are inconsistent with selfish aggrandisement, unjust suppression of our fellow-creatures, false worship, and false conduct to our brethren. Hence the Gospel of Unity, though it

RELIGION NOT A MOCKERY

V : 60

O ye who believe!
Take not for friends
And protectors those
Who take your religion
For a mockery or sport,—[194]
Whether among those
Who received the Scripture
Before you, or among those
Who reject Faith;
But fear ye God,
If ye have Faith (indeed).

RIGHTEOUSNESS—WHAT IT IS

II : 177

It is not righteousness
That ye turn your faces

is in complete accord with the pure pattern after which God made us, is yet hard to those who love self and falsehood. But Grace is free to all, and in His wise Plan, He will specially select Teachers to show the Way to humanity, and no one who turns to Him will lack guidance.

194. It is not right that we should be in intimate association with those to whom religion is either a subject of mockery or at best is nothing but a plaything. They may be amused, or they may have other motives for encouraging you. But your association with them will sap the earnestness of your Faith and make you cynical and insincere.

Towards East or West;
But it is righteousness—[195]
To believe in God [196]
And the Last Day,
And the Angels,
And the Book,
And the Messengers;
To spend of your substance,[197]
Out of love for Him,
For your kin,
For orphans,
For the needy,

195 As if to emphasize again a warning against deadening formalism, we are given a beautiful description of the righteous and God-fearing man. He should obey salutary regulations, but he should fix his gaze on the love of God and the love of his fellow-men. We are given four heads: (1) Our faith should be true and sincere; (2) we must be prepared to show it in deeds of charity to our fellow-men; (3) we must be good citizens, supporting social organization; and (4) our own individual soul must be firm and unshaken in all circumstances. They are interconnected, and yet can be viewed separately.

196. Faith is not merely a matter of words. We must realize the presence and goodness of God. When we do so, the scales fall from our eyes: all the falsities and fleeting nature of the Present cease to enslave us, for we see the Last Day as if it were to-day. We also see God's working in His world and in us: His Powers (angels), His Messengers and his Message are no longer remote from us, but come within our experience.

197. Practical deeds of charity are of value when they proceed from love, and from no other motive. In this respect, also, our duties take various forms, which are shown in reasonable gradation: our kith and kin; orphans (including any persons who are without support or help); people who are in real need but who never ask (it is our duty to find them out, and they come before those who ask); the stranger, who is entitled to laws of hospitality; the people who ask and are entitled to ask, *i.e.*, not merely lazy beggars, but those who seek our assistance in some form or another (it is our duty to respond to them); and the slaves (we must do all we can to give or buy their freedom). Slavery has many insidious forms, and all are included.

For the wayfarer,
For those who ask,
And for the ransom of slaves ;
To be steadfast in prayer,[198]
And practise regular charity ;
To fulfil the contracts
Which ye have made ;
And to be firm and patient[199]
In pain (or suffering)
And adversity,
And throughout
All periods of panic.
Such are the people
Of truth, the God-fearing.

THE RIGHTEOUS WILL INHERIT EARTH

XXI : 105 (part)

" My servants,
The righteous, shall inherit
The earth."

198. Charity and piety in individual cases do not complete our duties. In prayer and charity, we must also look to our organized efforts : where there is a Muslim State, these are made through the State, in facilities for public prayer, and public assistance, and for the maintenance of contracts, and fair dealing in all matters.

199. Then come the Muslim virtues of firmness and patience. They are to " preserve the dignity of man, with soul erect " (Burns). Three sets of circumstances are specially mentioned for the exercise of this virtue : (1) bodily pain or suffering. (2) adversities or injuries of all kinds. deserved and undeserved, and (3) periods of public panic, such as war, violence, pestilence, etc.

STRIVE

LIII : 39 to 41

39. That man can have nothing
But what he strives for;
40. That (the fruit of) his striving[200]
Will soon come in sight;
41. Then will he be rewarded
With a reward complete.

FULFIL (ALL) OBLIGATIONS

V : 1

O ye who believe!
Fulfil (all) obligations.[200-A]

TRUE ESTIMATE OF GOD—NO ONE CAN HAVE

XXII : 74

No just estimate have they
Made of God : for God
Is He Who is strong
And able to carry out

200. The second and third aphorisms are that man must strive, or he will gain nothing; and that if he strives, the result must soon appear in sight and he will find his reward in full measure.

200-A. This line has been justly admired for its terseness and comprehensiveness. Obligations : *uqud* : the Arabic word implies so many things that a whole chapter of Commentary

His Will.[201]

WILL, SOUL, WEALTH FOR GOD

IX : 111

God hath purchased of the Believers
Their persons and their goods;
For theirs (in return)
Is the Garden (of Paradise)[202]

can be written on it. First, there are the divine obligations that arise from our spiritual nature and our relation to God. He created us and implanted in us the faculty of knowledge and foresight; besides the intuition and reason which He gave us, He made Nature responsive to our needs, and His Signs in Nature are so many lessons to us in our own inner life; He further sent Messengers and Teachers, for the guidance of our conduct in individual, social, and public life. All these gifts create corresponding obligations, which we must fulfil. But in our own human and material life we undertake mutual obligations, express and implied. We make a promise; we enter into a commercial or social contract; we enter into a contract of marriage: we must faithfully fulfil all obligations in all these relationships. Our group or our state enters into a treaty: every individual in that group or state is bound to see that as far as lies in his power, such obligations are faithfully discharged. There are tacit obligations: living in civil society, we must respect its tacit conventions unless they are morally wrong, and in that case we must get out of such society. There are tacit obligations in the characters of host and guest, wayfarer or companion, employer or employed, ect., etc., which every man of Faith must discharge conscientiously. The man who deserts those who need him and goes to pray in a desert is a coward who disregards his obligations. All these obligations are interconnected. Truth and fidelity are parts of religion in all relations of life.

201. No one can have a true idea of God, who descends to the base forms or false worship. God has all power, and He is fully able to carry out every part of His Will and Plan. He is exalted above all in power and dignity.

202. In a human bargain both sides give something and receive some advantage. In the divine bargain of God with man, God takes man's will and soul and his wealth and goods, and

They fight in His Cause
And slay and are slain :
A promise binding on Him
In Truth, through the Law,
The Gospel, and the Quran : [203]
And who is more faithful
To His Covenant than God ?
Then rejoice in the bargain
Which ye have concluded :
That is the achievement supreme.

WHO ELSE BUT GOD LISTENS TO DISTRESSED SOUL

XXVII : 62

Or, who listens to the (soul)
Distressed when it calls

gives him in return everlasting Felicity. Man fights in God's Cause and carries out His will, the Universal Will. All that he has to give up is the ephemeral things of this world, while he gains eternal salvation, the fulfilment of his highest spiritual hopes,—a supreme achievement indeed.

203. We offer our whole selves and our possessions to God, and God gives us salvation, *i e.,* eternal freedom from the bondage of this world. This is the true doctrine of redemption ; and we are taught that this is the doctrine not only of the Quran but of earlier Revelations,—the original Law of Moses and the original Gospel of Jesus. Any other view of redemption is rejected by Islam, especially that of corrupted Christianity, which thinks that some other person suffered for our sins, and we are redeemed by his blood. It is our self-surrender that counts, not other people's merits. Our complete self-surrender may include fighting for the cause, both spiritual and physical. As regards actual fighting with the sword there has been some difference in theological theories at different times, but very little in the practice of those who framed those theories. The Jewish wars were ruthless wars of

On Him, and who relieves[204]
Its suffering, and makes you
(Mankind) inheritors of the earth ?
(Can there be another) god
Besides God ? Little it is
That ye heed !

WHOLE-HEARTEDLY ENTER IN ISLAM

II : 208 and 209

208. O ye who believe !
Enter into Islam
Whole-heartedly ;
And follow not
The footsteps
Of the Evil One ;
For he is to you
An avowed enemy.

extermination. The Old Testament does not mince matters on this subject. In the New Testament St. Paul, in commending the worthy fruits of Faith mentions Gideon, Barak, and other warriors of the Old Testament as his ideals, " Who through faith subdued kingdoms,.........waxed valiant in fight, turned to flight the armies of the aliens......" (Hebrews, XI. 32-34). The monkish morality of the Gospels in their present form has never been followed by any self-respecting Christian or other nation in history. Nor is it common-sense to ignore lust of blood in unregenerate man as a form of evil which has to be combated " within the limits set by God "

204. Besides the evidence of external nature, there is the still more intimate evidence in man's inner conscience and heart. God listens to man's cry of agony and relieves his suffering, and He has given him superiority over other creation on this earth, through his mind and soul. Is man then going to run after inferior beings and forget God ?

209 If ye backslide
After the clear (Signs)
Have come to you,
Then know that God
Is Exalted, Wise.[205]

WHAT IS LIFE OF THIS WORLD

XXIX : 64

What is the life of this world
But amusement and play?[206]
But verily the Home
In the Hereafter,—that is
Life indeed, if they but knew.

---

205. If you backslide after the conviction has been brought home to you, you may cause some inconvenience to the Cause, or to those who counted upon you, but do not be so arrogant as to suppose that you will defeat God's Power and Wisdom. The loss will be your own.

206. Amusement and play has no lasting significance except as preparing us for the serious work of life So this life is but an interlude, preparation for the real Life, which is in the Hereafter. This world's vanities are therefore to be taken for what they are worth ; but they are not to be allowed to deflect our minds from the requirements of the inner life that really matters.

IV.—FASTING

II : 183

O ye who believe!
Fasting is prescribed to you
As it was prescribed [207]
To those before you,
That ye may (learn)
Self-restraint,—

II : 185

Ramadhan is the month
In which was sent down
The Quran, as a guide
To mankind, also clear (Signs)
For guidance and judgment [208]
(Between right and wrong).
So every one of you
Who is present (at his home)
During that month
Should spend it in fasting,
But if any one is ill,
Or on a journey,

207. *As it was prescribed*: this does not mean that the Muslim fast is like the other fasts previously observed, in the number of days, in the time or manner of the fast, or in other incidents; it only means that the principle of self-denial by fasting is not a new one.

208. Judgment (between right and wrong): *Furqan*=the criterion or standard by which we judge between right and wrong.

The prescribed period
(Should be made up)
By days later.
God intends every facility
For you; He does not want
To put you to difficulties.
He wants you to complete
The prescribed period,
And to glorify Him[209]
In that He has guided you;
And perchance ye shall be grateful.

II : 187

Permitted to you,
On the night of the fasts,
Is the approach to your wives.
They are your garments
And ye are their garments.[210]
God knoweth what ye
Used to do secretly among yourselves;
But He turned to you

209. The regulations are again and again coupled with an insistence on two things: (*a*) the facilities and concessions given, and (*b*) the spiritual significance of the fast, without which it is like an empty shell without a kernel. If we realize this, we shall look upon Ramadhan, not as a burden, but as a blessing, and shall be duly grateful for the lead given to us in this matter.

210. Men and women are each other's garments: *i.e.* they are for mutual support, mutual comfort, and mutual protection, fitting into each other as a garment fits the body. A garment also is both for show and concealment. The question of sex is always delicate to handle: here we are told that even in such matters a clear, open, and honest course is better than fraud or self-deception. The sex instinct is classed with eating and drinking, an animal thing to be restrained, but not to be ashamed of. The three things are prohibited during the fast by day but permitted after the fast is broken at night till the next fast commences.

And forgave you;
So now associate with them,
And seek what God
Hath ordained for you,[211]
And eat and drink,
Until the white thread
Of dawn appear to you
Distinct from its black thread;[212]
Then complete your fast
Till the night appears;[213]
But do not associate
With your wives
While ye are in retreat[214]
In the mosques. Those are[215]
Limits (set by) God:
Approach not nigh thereto.
Thus doth God make clear
His Signs to men: that
They may learn self-restraint.

211. There is difference of opinion as to the exact meaning of this. I would connect this as a parallel clause with the clause, "eat and drink," which follows, all three being governed by "until the white thread," etc. That is, all three things must stop when the fast begins again in the early morning. Or it may mean: What is permitted is well enough, but seek the higher things ordained for you.

212. Those in touch with Nature know the beautiful effects of early dawn. First appear thin white indefinable streaks of light in the east; then a dark zone supervenes; followed by a beautiful pinkish white zone clearly defined from the dark. This is the true dawn; after that the fast begins.

213. *Till the night appears*: From the actual practice of the Holy Apostle, this is rightly interpreted to mean: "Till sunset."

214. Retreat to the Mosques by night after the fast is broken is specially recommended towards the end of Ramadhan so that all carnal temptations may be avoided.

215. I construe these limits as applying to the whole of the regulations about fasts.

V.—FOOD

WHAT TO EAT

II : 172

O ye who believe !
Eat of the good things
That We have provided for you,
And be grateful to God,
If it is Him ye worship.[216]

V : 6

This day are all things
Good and pure made lawful
Unto you. The food
Of the People of the Book,[217]
Is lawful unto you
And yours is lawful
Unto them.
(Lawful unto you in marriage)
Are (not only) chaste women
Who are believers, but

216. Gratitude for God's gifts is one form of worship.

217. The question is for food generally, such as is ordinarily "good and pure" in the matter of meat it should be killed with some sort of solemnity analogous to that of the *kalima*. The rules of Islam in this respect being analogous to those of the People of the Book, there is no objection to mutual recognition, as opposed to meat killed by Pagans with superstitious rites.

Chaste women among
The People of the Book,[218]
Revealed before your time,—
When ye give them
Their due dowers, and desire
Chastity, not lewdness,
Nor secret intrigues.
If any one rejects faith,[219]
Fruitless will be his work,
And in the Hereafter
He will be in the ranks
Of those who have lost
(All spiritual good).

XVI : 114 and 115

114. So eat of the sustenance
Which God has provided

In this respect the Christian rule is the same : "That ye abstain from meats offered to idols, and from blood, and from things strangled, and from fornication." Notice the bracketing of fornication with things unlawful to eat.

218. Islam is not exclusive. Social intercourse, including inter marriage, is permitted with the People of the Book. A Muslim man may marry a woman from their ranks on the same terms as he would marry a Muslim woman, *i.e.*, he must give her an economic and moral status, and must not be actuated merely by motives of lust or physical desire. A Muslim woman may not marry a non-Muslim man, because her Muslim status would be affected : the wife ordinarily takes the nationality and status given by her husband's law. A non-Muslim woman marrying a Muslim husband would be expected eventually to accept Islam. Any man or woman, of any race or faith, may, on accepting Islam, freely marry any Muslim woman or man, provided it be from motives of purity and chastity and not of lewdness.

219. As always, food, cleanliness, social intercourse, marriage and other interests in life, are linked with our duty to God and faith in Him. Duty and faith are for our own benefit, here and in the Hereafter.

For you, lawful and good;
And be grateful for the favours [220]
Of God, if it is He
Whom Ye serve.
115. He has only forbidden you
Carrion, and blood,
And the flesh of swine,
And any (food) over which
The name of other than God
Has been invoked.
But if one is forced by necessity,
Without wilful disobedience,
Nor transgressing due limits,—
Then God is Oft-forgiving,
Most Merciful.

V : 90

O ye who believe!
Make not unlawful
The good things which God
Hath made lawful for you,
But commit no excess: [221]

220. Ingratitude for God's sustenance (in the literal and figurative senses) may be shown in various ways: *e.g.*, (1) by forgetting or refusing to acknowledge the true source of the bounty, *viz.*, God, (2) by misusing or misapplying the bounty, as by committing excesses in things lawful, or refusing to share them with others of God's creatures when the need arises, (3) by falsely ascribing to God any prohibitions we may set up for ourselves for special reasons or because of our special idiosyncracies.

221. In pleasures that are good and lawful the crime is excess. There is no merit merely in abstention or asceticism, though the humility or unselfishness that may go with asceticism may have its value. Christian monks are praised for particular virtues, though here and elsewhere monasticism

For God loveth not
Those given to excess.

WHAT NOT TO EAT

V : 4 (part)

Forbidden to you (for food)
Are : carrion, blood,
The flesh of swine, and that
On which hath been invoked
The name of other than God ; [222]
That which hath been
Killed by strangling,
Or by a violent blow,
Or by a headlong fall,
Or by being gored to death ;
That which hath been (partly)
Eaten by a wild animal ;
Unless ye are able
To slaughter it (in due form) ; [223]
That which is sacrificed
On stone (altars) ;

is disapproved of. Use God's gifts of all kinds with gratitude, but excess is not approved of by God.

222. The prohibition of carrion, blood, the flesh of swine, and that on which other names than that of God has been invoked, has been explained. If an animal dies by strangling, or by a violent blow, or a headlong fall, or by being gored to death, or by being attacked by a wild animal, the presumption is that it becomes carrion, as the life-blood is congealed before being taken out of the body. But the presumption can be rebutted. If the life-blood still flows and the solemn mode of slaughter (*zabh*) in the name of God as a sacrifice is carried out, it becomes lawful as food.

223. This was also an idolatrous rite, different from that in which a sacrifice was devoted to a particular idol or a false god.

(Forbidden) also is the division
(Of meat) by raffling
With arrows : that is impiety.

VI : 121

Eat not of (meats)
On which God's name
Hath not been pronounced :
That would be impiety.
But the evil ones
Ever inspire their friends
To contend with you.
If ye were to obey them,
Ye would indeed be Pagans.

VI : 145

Say : " I find not
In the Message received
By me by inspiration
Any (meat) forbidden
To be eaten by one
Who wishes to eat it,
Unless it be carrion,
Or blood poured forth,[224]
Or the flesh of swine,—
For it is an abomination—
Or, what is impious, (meat)
On which a name has been
Invoked, other than God's."
But (even so), if a person

224. *Blood poured forth* : as distinguished from blood adhering to flesh, or the liver, or such other internal organs purifying the blood.

Is forced by necessity,
Without wilful disobedience,
Nor transgressing due limits,—
Thy Lord is Oft-forgiving,
Most Merciful.

II : 173

He hath only forbidden you
Carrion,[225] and blood,
And the flesh of swine,
And that on which
Any other name hath been invoked
Besides that of God.[226]
But if one is forced by necessity,
Without wilful disobedience,
Nor transgressing due limits,—
Then is he guiltless.
For God is Oft-forgiving
Most Merciful.

225. Carrion : *maitat* : the original Arabic has a slightly wider meaning given to it in *Fiqah* (Religious Law) : anything that dies of itself, *i.e.*, which is not expressly killed for food with the *Kalima* duly pronounced on it. But there are exceptions, *e.g.*, fish and locusts are lawful, though they have not been made specially *halal* with the *Kalima*. But even fish or locusts as carrion would be obviously ruled out.

226. The teachers of *Fiqh* (Religions Law) work out the details with great elaboration. My purpose is to present general principles, not technical details. Carrion and blood as articles of food would obviously cause disgust to any refined person. So would swine's flesh where the swine live on offal. Where swine are fed artificially on clean food, the objections remain : (1) that they are filthy animals in other respects, and the flesh of filthy animals taken as food affects the eater ; (2) that swine's flesh has more fat than muscle building material ; and (3) that it is more liable to disease than other kinds of meat ; *e.g.*, trichinosis, characterized by hair-like worms in the muscular tissue. As to food dedicated to idols or false gods, it is obviously unseemly for the Children of Unity to partake of it.

VI.—HAJ (PILGRIMAGE)

II : 197

For *Hajj*
Are the months well-known.[227]
If any one undertakes
That duty therein,
Let there be no obscenity,
Nor wickedness,

227. *The months well-known*: the months of *Shawwal*, *Zulqad*, and *Zul-hajj* (up to the 10th or the 13th) are set apart for the rites of *Hajj*. That is to say, the first rites may begin as early as the beginning of *Shawwal*, with a definite approach to Mecca, but the chief rites are concentrated on the first ten days of *Zul-Hajj*, and specially on the 8th, 9th and 10th of that month, when the concourse of pilgrims reaches its height. The chief rites may be briefly enumerated: (1) The wearing of the pilgrim garment (*ihram*) from certain points definitely fixed on all the roads to Mecca; after this the pilgrimage prohibitions come into operation and the pilgrim is dedicated to worship and prayer and the denial of vanities; (2) the going round the Ka'ba seven times (*tawaf*), typifying activity, with the kissing of the little Black Stone built into the wall, the symbol of concentration in the love of God; (3) after a short prayer at the Station of Abraham, the pilgrim goes to the hills Safa and Marwa, the symbols of patience and perseverance: (4) the great Sermon (*Khutba*) on the 7th of *Zulhajj*, when the whole assembly listens to an exposition of the meaning of *Hajj*; (5) the visit on the eighth, of the whole body of pilgrims to the Valley of Mina (about six miles north of Mecca), where the pilgrims halt and stay the night, proceeding on the 9th to the plain and hill of Arafat, about five miles further north, which commemorates the reunion of Adam and Eve after their wanderings, and is also called the Mount of Mercy; (6) the tenth day, the Id Day, the day of Sacrifice, when the sacrifice is offered in the Valley of Mina, and the symbolic ceremony of casting seven stones at the Evil One is performed on the first occasion; it is continued on subsequent days; both rites are connected with the story of Abraham: this is the Id-ul-Adhha; note that the ceremony is symbolically connected with the rejection of evil in thought, word, and deed. This closes the pilgrimage, but a stay of two or three days after this is recommended, and this is called *Tashriq*.

Nor wrangling
In the *Hajj*.
And whatever good
Ye do, (be sure)
God knoweth it.
And take a provision [228]
(With you) for the journey,
But the best of provisions
Is right conduct.
So fear Me,
O ye that are wise.

---

228. It is recommended that pilgrims should come with provisions, so that they should not be compelled to resort to begging. But, as usual, our thought is directed at once from the physical to the spiritual. If provisions are required for a journey on earth, how much more important to provide for the final journey into the future world? The best of such provisions is right conduct, which is the same as the fear of God.

VII.—FIGHTING IN THE CAUSE OF GOD (JIHAD)

DEAL JUSTLY

LX : 8

God forbids you not,
With regard to those who
Fight you not for (your) Faith
Nor drive you out
Of your homes,
From dealing kindly and justly [229]
With them : for God loveth
Those who are just.

DO NOT TRANSGRESS

II : 190

Fight in the cause of God
Those who fight you,[230]

229. Even with Unbelievers, unless they are rampant and out to destroy us and our Faith, we should deal kindly and equitably, as is shown by our Holy Prophet's own example.

230. War is only permissible in self-defence, and under well-defined limits. When undertaken, it must be pushed with vigour, but not relentlessly, but only to restore peace and freedom for the worship of God. In any case strict limits must not be transgressed : women, children, old and infirm men should not be molested, nor trees and crops cut down, nor peace withheld when the enemy comes to terms.

But do not transgress limits;
For God loveth not transgressors.

DO NOT BE AFRAID OF DEATH

III:156

O ye who believe!
Be not like the Unbelievers,
Who say of their brethren,
When they are travelling
Through the earth or engaged
In fighting: "If they had stayed
With us, they would not
Have died, or been slain."
This that God may make it
A cause of sighs and regrets
In their hearts. It is God
That gives Life and Death,[231]

231. It is want of faith that makes people afraid (1) of meeting death, (2) of doing their duty when it involves danger, as in travelling in order to earn an honest living, or fighting in a sacred cause. Such fear is part of the punishment for want of faith. If you have faith, there is no fear in meeting death, for it brings you nearer to your goal, nor in meeting danger for a sufficient cause, because you know that the keys of life and death are in God's hands. Nothing can happen without God's Will. If it is God's Will that you should die, your staying at home will not save you. If it is God's Will that you should live, the danger you incur in a just cause brings you glory. Supposing it is His Will that you should lose your life in the danger, there are three considerations that would make you eager to meet it: (1) dying in doing your duty is the best means of reaching God's Mercy; (2) the man of faith knows that he is not going to an unknown country of which he has no news; he is going nearer to God; and (3) he is being "brought together" unto God; *i.e.*, he will meet all his dear ones in faith: instead of the separation which the souls without faith fear, he looks forward to a surer reunion than is possible in this life.

And God sees well
All that ye do.

NO HOSTILITY

II : 193

And fight them on
Until there is no more
Tumult or oppression,
And there prevail
Justice and faith in God;[232]
But if they cease,[233]
Let there be no hostility
Except to those
Who practise oppression.

PEACE

VIII : 61

But if the enemy
Incline towards peace,
Do thou (also) incline
Towards peace, and trust

232. *Justice and faith.* The Arabic word is *Dīn*, which is comprehensive. It implies the ideas of indebtedness, duty, obedience, judgment, justice, faith, religion, customary rites, etc. The clause means : "Until there is *Dīn* for God."

233. If the opposite party, cease to persecute you, your hostility ends with them as a party, but it does not mean that you become friends to oppression. Your fight is against wrong; there should be no rancour against men.

In God : for He is the One
That heareth and knoweth
(All things).[234]

REASONS WHY FIGHTING (JIHAD) PRESCRIBED

IV : 75

And why should ye not
Fight in the cause of God
And of those who, being weak,[235]
Are ill-treated (and oppressed) ?—
Men, women, and children,
Whose cry is : "Our Lord !
Rescue us from this town,
Whose people are oppressors ;
And raise for us from Thee
One who will protect,
One who will help !"[236]

234. While we must always be ready for the good fight lest it be forced on us, even in the midst of the fight we must always be ready for peace if there is any inclination towards peace on the other side. There is no merit merely in a fight by itself. It should be a joyful duty not for itself, but to establish the reign of peace and righteousness and God's Law.

235. Mustadha=one reckoned weak and therefore ill-treated and oppressed.

236. Even from the human point of view the cause of God is the cause of justice, the cause of the oppressed. In the great persecution, before Mecca was won again, what sorrows, threats, tortures, and oppressions, were suffered by those whose faith was unshaken? Muhammad's life and that of his adherents was threatened : they were mocked, assaulted, insulted and beaten ; those within the power of the enemy were put into chains and cast into prison ; others were boycotted, and shut out of trade, business and social intercourse ; they could not even buy the

II : 216

Fighting is prescribed
For you, and ye dislike it.[237]
But it is possible
That ye dislike a thing
Which is good for you,
And that ye love a thing
Which is bad for you.
But God knoweth
And ye know not.

III : 146

How many of the Prophets
Fought (in God's way),
And with them (fought)
Large bands of godly men?
But they never lost heart
If they met with disaster
In God's way, nor did
They weaken (in will)
Nor give in. For God
Loves those who are

food they wanted, or performed their religious duties. The persecution was redoubled for the believing slaves, women, and children after the Hijrat. Their cry for a protector and helper from God was answered when Muhammad the Chosen One brought freedom and peace to Mecca again.

237. To fight in the cause of Truth is one of the highest forms of charity. What can you offer that is more precious than your own life? But here again the limitations come in. If you are a mere brawler, or a selfish aggressive person, or a vainglorious bully, you deserve the highest censure. If you offer your life to the righteous Imam, who is only guided by God, you are an unselfish hero. God knows the value of things better than you do.

Firm and steadfast.

II : 191

And slay them
Wherever ye catch them,
And turn them out
From where they have
Turned you out;
For tumult and oppression
Are worse than slaughter;
But fight them not[238]
At the Sacred Mosque,
Unless they (first)

238. This passage is illustrated by the events that happened at Hudaibiya in the sixth year of the Hijra, though it is not clear that it was revealed on that occasion. The Muslims were by this time a strong and influential community. Many of them were exiles from Mecca, where the Pagans had established an intolerant autocracy, persecuting Muslims, preventing them from visiting their homes and even keeping them out by force from performing the Pilgrimage during the universally recognized period of truce. This was intolerance, oppression, and autocracy to the last degree, and the mere readiness of the Muslims to enforce their rights as Arab citizens resulted without bloodshed in an agreement which the Muslims faithfully observed. The pagans, however, had no scruples in breaking faith, and it is unnecessary here to go into subsequent events.

In general, it may be said that Islam is the religion of peace, goodwill, mutual understanding and good faith. But it will not acquiesce in wrong-doing, and its men will hold their lives cheap in defence of honour, justice, and the religion which they hold sacred. Their ideal is that of heroic virtue combined with unselfish gentleness and tenderness, such as is exemplified in the life of the Apostle. They believe in courage, obedience, discipline, duty, and a constant striving, by all the means in their power, physical, moral, intellectual and spiritual, for the establishment of truth and righteousness. They know that war is an evil, but they will not flinch from it if their honour demands it, and (*a most important condition*) a righteous *Imam* (such as Muhammad was *par excellence*) commands it, for then they know they are not serving carnal ends. In other cases, war has nothing to do with their faith, except that it will always be regulated by its human precepts.

Fight you there;
But if they fight you,
Slay them.
Such is the reward
Of those who suppress faith.

XXII : 39 and 40

39. To those against him whom[239]
War is made, permission
Is given (to fight), because
They are wronged;—and verily,
God is Most Powerful
For their aid;—
40. (They are) those who have
Been expelled from their homes
In defiance of right,—
(For no cause) except
That they say, "Our Lord
Is God." Did not God
Check one set of people
By means of another,[240]

239. Several translators have failed to notice that *yuqataluna* (in the best approved texts) is in the passive voice, "against whom war is made,"— not "who take arms against the unbelievers" as Sale translates it. The clause "and verily...their aid" is parenthetical. Verse 40 connects on with "they are wronged." The wrong is indicated: "driven by persecution from their home, for no other reason than that they worshipped the One True God." This was the first occasion on which fighting—in self-defence—was permitted. This passage therefore undoubtedly dates from Medina.

240. Where the expression is used in connection with David's fight against the Philistines. To allow a righteous people to fight against a ferocious and mischief-loving people was fully justified. But the justification was far greater here, when the little Muslim community was not only fighting for its own existence against the Meccan Quraish, but for the

There would surely have been
Pulled down monasteries, churches,
Synagogues, and mosques, in which
The name of God is commemorated
In abundant measure. God will
Certainly aid those who
Aid His (cause);—for verily
God is Full of Strength,
Exalted in Might,[241]
(Able to enforce His Will).

SLAIN IN THE WAY OF GOD THEIR DEEDS ARE NOT LOST

III : 169 to 171

169. Think not of those
Who are slain in God's way
As dead. Nay, they live,[242]
Finding their sustenance
In the Presence of their Lord;

very existence of the Faith in the One True God. They had as much right to be in Mecca and worship in the Ka'ba as the other Quraish; yet they were exiled for their Faith. It affected not the faith of one peculiar people. The principle involved was that of all worship, Jewish or Christian as well as Muslim, and of all foundations built for pious uses.

241. *Aziz* means Exalted in power, rank, dignity; Incomparable; full of might and majesty; able to enforce His Will. The last signification is the one that predominates here.

242. A beautiful passage about the Martyrs in the cause of Truth. They are not dead: they live,—and in a far higher and deeper sense than in the life they have left. Even those who have no faith in the Hereafter honour those that die in their cause, with the crown of immortality in the minds and memories of generations unborn. But in Faith we see a higher,

170. They rejoice in the Bounty
Provided by God:
And with regard to those
Left behind, who have not
Yet joined them (in their bliss),
The (Martyrs) glory in the fact
That on them is no fear,
Nor have they cause to grieve.[243]
171. They glory in the Grace
And the Bounty from God,
And in the fact that
God suffereth not
The reward of the Faithful
To be lost (in the least).

IV : 74

Let those fight
In the cause of God

truer, and less relative immortality. Perhaps "immortality" is not the right word in this connection, as it implies a continuation of this life. In their case, through the gateway of death, they enter the true real Life, as opposed to its shadow here. Our carnal life is sustained with carnal food, and its joys and pleasures at their best are those which are projected on the screen of this material world. Their real Life is sustained from the ineffable Presence and Nearness of God.

243. The Martyrs not only rejoice at the bliss they have themselves attained. The dear ones left behind are in their thoughts: it is part of their glory that they have saved their dear ones from fear, sorrow, humiliation, and grief, in this life, even before they come to share in the glories of the Hereafter. Note how the refrain: "on them shall be no fear, nor shall they grieve": comes in here with a new and appropriate meaning. Besides other things, it means that the dear ones have no cause to grieve at the death of the Martyrs; rather have they cause to rejoice.

Who sell the life of this world
For the Hereafter,[244]
To him who fighteth
In the cause of God,—
Whether he is slain
Or gets victory—
Soon shall We give him
A reward of great (value).

XLVII : 4

Therefore, when ye meet [245]
The Unbelievers (in fight),
Smite at their necks ;
At length, when ye have
Thoroughly subdued them,
Bind a bond [246]

244. It is not every one least of all, poltroons and faint-hearted persons—who is fit to fight in the cause of God. To do so is a privilege, and those who understand the privilege are prepared to sacrifice all their interests in this life, and this life itself ; for they know that it is the sacrifice of something fleeting and of little value, for the sake of something everlasting, and of immense value. Whether (in appearance) they win or lose, in reality they win the prize for which they are fighting, *viz*., honour and glory in the sight of God. Note that the only alternatives here are Death or Victory ! The true fighter knows no defeat.

245. When once the fight (*Jihad*) is entered upon, carry it out with the utmost vigour, and strike home your blows at the most vital points (*smite at their necks*) both literally and figuratively. You cannot wage war with kid gloves.

246. In the first onset there must necessarily be great loss of life ; but when the enemy is fairly beaten, which means, in a Jihad that he is not likely to seek again the persecution of Truth, firm arrangements should be made to bring him under control. I thus construe the words "bind a bond firmly (on them)", but others have construed the words to mean, "after the enemy's numbers are fairly thinned down, prisoners may be taken."

Firmly (on them) : thereafter
(Is the time for) either
Generosity or ransom : [247]
Until the war lays down
Its burdens. Thus (are ye
Commanded) : but if it
Had been God's Will,
He could certainly have exacted
Retribution from them (Himself);
But (He lets you fight)
In order to test you, [248]
Some with others.
But those who are slain [249]
In the way of God,—
He will never let
Their deeds be lost.

---

247. When once the enemy is brought under control generosity (*i.e.*, the release of prisoners without ransom) or ransom is recommended

248. The believers are tested in Faith by the extent to which they are willing to make sacrifices, even to the laying down of their lives ; and the enemies are tested as to whether they would repent and let the righteous live in freedom and security.

249. There are two alternative readings, (1) *qatalu* "those who fight," and (2) *qutilu*, "those who are slain." The meaning under the first reading is wider and includes that under the second. I have translated on the basis of the second reading, which is in accordance with the text of the Royal Egyptian edition.

VIII.—PRAYER (NAMAZ)

ABLUTION

V : 7

O ye who believe !
When ye prepare
For prayer, wash[250]
Your faces, and your hands
(And arms) to the elbows;
Rub your heads (with water);
And (wash) your feet
To the ankles.
If ye are in a state
Of ceremonial impurity,[251]
Bathe your whole body.
But if ye are ill,
Or on a journey,
Or one of you cometh
From offices of nature,
Or ye have been
In contact with women,
And ye find no water,

250. These are the essentials of Wudhu, or ablutions preparatory to prayers, *viz.*: (1) to bathe the whole face in water, and (2) both hands and arms to the elbows, with (3) a little rubbing of the head with water (as the head is usually protected and comparatively clean), and (4) the bathing of the feet to the ankles. In addition following the practice of the Apostle, it is usual first to wash the mouth, the throat, and the nose, before proceeding with the face, etc.

251. Ceremonial impurity arises from sex pollution.

Then take for yourselves
Clean sand or earth,[252]
And rub therewith
Your faces and hands.
God doth not wish
To place you in a difficulty,
But to make you clean,
And to complete
His favour to you,
That ye may be grateful.

IV : 43

O ye who believe!
Approach not prayers
With a mind befogged,[253]
Until ye can understand
All that ye say,—
Nor in a state
Of ceremonial impurity
(Except when travelling on the road),
Until after washing
Your whole body.

252. This is *Tayammum* or washing with clean sand or earth where water is not available. I take it that this substitute is permissible both for Wudhu and for a full bath in the circumstances mentioned.

253. The reference is either to a state of intoxication or to a dazed state of mind on account of drowsiness or some other cause. Or perhaps both are implied. Before the prohibition of intoxicants altogether was promulgated, it was at least unbecoming that people should come to prayers in such a state. For prayers it is only right that we should collect our whole minds and approach God in a spirit of reverence. "Prayers" (*Salat*) here may mean "a place of prayers", a Mosque: the resulting meaning would be the same.

If ye are ill,
Or on a journey,
Or one of you cometh
From offices of nature,
Or ye have been
In contact with women,
And ye find no water,[254]
Then take for yourselves
Clean sand or earth,
And rub therewith
Your faces and hands.
For God doth blot out sins
And forgive again and again.

LXXIV : 4

Thy raiment purify.

ADORE LORD

II : 21

O ye people!
Adore your Guardian-Lord,
Who created you
And those who came before you,

254. The strictest cleanliness and purity of mind and body are required, especially at the time of prayer. But there are circumstances when water for ablutions is not easily obtainable, especially in the dry conditions of Arabia, and then washing with dry sand or clean earth is recommended. Four such circumstances are mentioned: the two last when washing is specially required; the two first when washing may be necessary, but it may not be easy to get water. For a man, when he is ill, cannot walk out far to get water, and a man on a journey has no full control over his supplies. In all four cases, where water cannot be got, cleaning with dry sand or dry earth is recommended. This is called *Tayammum*.

That ye may have the chance
To learn righteousness.[255]

BE STEADFAST

II : 42 and 43

And cover not Truth
With falsehood, nor conceal
The truth when ye know (what it is).
43. And be steadfast in prayer;[256]
Practise regular charity;
And bow down your heads
With those who bow down (in worship).

CALL LORD

XL : 60

And your Lord says:
" Call on Me; I

255. I connect this dependent clause with "adore, etc.," above, though it could be connected with "created". According to my construction the argument will be as follows. Adoration is the act of the highest and humblest reverence and worship. When you get into that relationship with God, who is your Creator and Guardian, your faith produces works of righteousness. It is a chance given you: will you exercise your free will and take it? If you do, your whole nature will be transformed.

256. The argument is still primarily addressed to the Jews, but is of universal application; as in all the teachings of the Quran. The chief feature of the Jewish worship was and is the bowing of the head.

Will answer (your Prayer) : [257]
But those who are
Too arrogant to serve Me
Will surely find themselves
In Hell—in humiliation !"

DURING WAR AND OUT OF DANGER

IV : 102 and 103

102. When thou (O Apostle)
Art with them, and standest
To lead them in prayer,
Let one party of them
Stand up (in prayer) with thee,
Taking their arms with them :
When they finish
Their prostrations, let them
Take their position in the rear,
And let the other party come up—
Which hath not yet prayed—
And let them pray with thee,
Taking all precautions,
And bearing arms :
The Unbelievers wish,
If ye were negligent
Of your arms and your baggage,
To assault you in a single rush. [258]

257. As this life is not the end of all things, and we are to have its fulfilment in the Hereafter : we have only to pray to the Lord of the Present and the Hereafter, and He will hear us, forgive us, guide us, and make our Path smooth. But Pride will have its fall,—and its humiliating Punishment.

258. The congregational prayer in danger in face of the

But there is no blame on you
If ye put away your arms
Because of the inconvenience
Of rain or because ye are ill ;
But take (every) precaution
For yourselves. For the Unbelievers
God hath prepared
A humiliating punishment.

103. When ye pass[259]
(Congregational) prayers,
Celebrate God's praises,
Standing, sitting down,
Or lying down on your sides ;
But when ye are free
From danger, set up
Regular Prayers :
For such prayers
Are enjoined on Believers
At stated times.

enemy rests on the principle that the congregation should be divided into two parties ; one party prays while the other watches the enemy, and then the second party comes up to prayers while the first falls back to face the enemy; either party does only one or two Rakats, or about half the congregational prayer; every precaution is taken to prevent a rush by the enemy; even while at prayers armour and arms need not be put off except when rain is likely to cause inconvenience to the wearer and damage to the arms, or when illness or fatigue causes the wearer's strength to fail. Details can be varied according to circumstances, as was actually done by the Apostle at different times.

259. Two interpretations are possible: (1) "When ye have finished congregational prayers", or (2) "When (on account of extreme danger) ye have to pass over congregational prayers altogether,—even the shorter form indicated for times of danger". I prefer the latter, as it accords better with the following sentence, which allows you to remember God individually in any posture possible during the danger. But when the danger is past, the full prayers should be offered at the stated times.

ENJOIN YOUR PEOPLE TO PRAY

XX : 132

Enjoin prayer on thy people,
And be constant therein.
We ask thee not to provide[260]
Sustenance; We provide it
For thee. But the (fruit of)
The Hereafter is for Righteousness.

FORMS OF PRAYER

I : 1 to 7

Fatiha, or the Opening Chapter.[261]

1. *In the name of God, Most Gracious Most Merciful.*[262]

260. Sustenance, in the sense of the ordinary needs of life, the man of God does not worry about. That is provided by God for all, the just and the unjust. But the special provision, the real Sustenance, the spiritual fruit, is for a righteous life in the service of God.

261. By universal consent it is rightly placed at the beginning of the Quran, as summing up, in marvellously terse and comprehensive words, man's relation to God in contemplation and prayer. In our spiritual contemplation the first words should be those of praise. If the praise is from our inmost being it brings us into union with God's will. Then our eyes see all good, peace and harmony. Evil, rebellion, and conflict are purged out. They do not exist for us, for our eyes are lifted up, above them in praise. Then we see God's attributes better (verses 2-4). This leads us to the attitude of worship and acknowledgment (verse 5) and finally comes prayer for guidance, and a contemplation of what guidance means (verses 6-7).

God needs no praise, for He is above all praise; He needs no petition, for He knows our needs better than we do ourselves: and His bounties are open without asking, to the righteous and the sinner alike. The prayer is for our own spiritual education, consolation and confirmation.

That is why the words in this Sura are given to us in the form in which we should utter them. When we reach enlightenment, they flow spontaneously from us.

262. The Arabic words *Rahman* and *Rahim* translated "Most Gracious" and "Most Merciful" are both intensive forms referring to different aspects of God's attribute of Mercy. The

2. Praise be to God,
The Cherisher and Sustainer[263] of the Worlds;
3 Most Gracious, Most Merciful;
4. Ruler of the Day of Judgment.
5. Thee do we worship,[264]
And Thine aid we seek.
6. Show[265] us the straight Way,

Arabic intensive is more suited to express God's attributes than the superlative degree in English. The latter implies a comparison with other beings, or with other times or places, while there is no being like unto God, and He is independent of Time and Place. Mercy may imply pity, long suffering, patience, and forgiveness, all of which the sinner needs, and God Most Merciful bestows in abundant measure. But there is a Mercy that goes before even the need arises, the Grace which is ever watchful, and flows from God Most Gracious to all His creatures, protecting them, preserving them, guiding them and leading them to clearer light and higher life. To make us contemplate these boundless gifts of God, the formula: "In the name of God, Most Gracious, Most Merciful": is placed before every Sura of the Quran (except the ninth) and repeated at the beginning of every act by the Muslim who dedicates his life to God, and whose hope is in His Mercy.

263. The Arabic word *Rabb* usually translated Lord, has also the meaning of cherishing, sustaining bringing to maturity. God cares for all the worlds He has created. There are many worlds,—astronomical and physical worlds, worlds of thought, spiritual worlds, and so on. In every one of them, God is all in all. We express only one aspect of it when we say: "In Him we live, and move and have our being."

264. On realizing in our souls God's love and care, His Grace and Mercy, and his Power and Justice (as Ruler of the Day of Judgment), the immediate result is that we bend in the act of worship, and see both our shortcomings and His All-sufficient power. The emphatic form means that not only do we reach the position of worshipping God and asking for His help, but we worship Him alone and ask for His aid only For there is none other than He worthy of our devotion and able to help us The plural "we" indicates that we associate ourselves with all who seek God, thus strengthening ourselves and strengthening them in a fellowship of faith.

265. If we translate by the English word "Guide," we shall have to say: "Guide us to and in the straight Way." For we may

7. The way of those on whom
Thou hast bestowed Thy Grace,
Not of those
Whose portion is Wrath[266]
Nor of those who stray.[267]

II : 286 (part).—Prayer

(Pray :) " Our Lord !
Condemn us not
If we forget or fall
Into error ; our Lord !
Lay not on us a burden
Like that which Thou

be wandering aimlessly, and the first step is to find the Way ; and the second need is to keep in the Way : our own wisdom may fail in either case. The straight Way is often the narrow Way or the steep Way, which many people shun. By the world's perversity the straight Way is sometimes stigmatized and the crooked Way praised. How are we to judge ? We must ask for God's guidance. With a little spiritual insight we shall see which are the people who walk in the light of God's grace, and which are those that walk in the darkness of Wrath. This also would help our judgment.

266. Note that the words relating to Grace are connected actively with God ; those relating to Wrath are impersonal. In the one case God's Mercy encompasses us beyond our deserts. In the other case our own actions are responsible for the Wrath,—the negative of Grace, Peace or Harmony.

267. Are there two categories ?—those who are in the darkness of Wrath and those who stray ? If so, the first are in greater spiritual danger than the second. The first are those who deliberately break God's law ; the second those who stray out of carelessness or negligence. Both are responsible for their own acts or omissions. In opposition to both are the people who are in the light of God's Grace : for His Grace not only protects them from active wrong (if they will only submit their will to Him) but also from straying into paths of temptation or carelessness.

Didst lay on those before us; [268]
Our Lord! lay not on us
A burden greater than we
Have strength to bear.
Blot out our sins,
And grant us forgiveness.
Have mercy on us.
Thou art our Protector;
Help us against those
Who stand against Faith."

III : 8.—Prayer

"Our Lord!" they say,
"Let not our hearts deviate
Now after Thou has guided us,
But grant us mercy
From Thine own Presence;
For Thou art the Grantor
Of bounties without measure.

III : 15 (end), 16 and 17

15. For in God's sight
Are (all) His servants,—

268. We must not be arrogant, and think that because God has granted us His favour and mercy we have no need to exert ourselves, or that we are ourselves superior to those before us. On the contrary, knowing how much they failed, we pray that our burdens should be lightened, and we confess our realization that we have all the greater need for God's mercy and forgiveness.

And so we end the whole argument of the Sura with a prayer for God's help, not in our own selfish ends, but in our resolve to uphold God's truth against all Unbelief.

16. Namely, those who say:
" Our Lord! we have indeed
Believed: forgive us, then,
Our sins. and save us
From the agony of the Fire;"—
17. Those who show patience,
Firmness and self-control:[269]
Who are true (in word and deed);
Who worship devoutly;
Who spend (in the way of God);
And who pray for forgiveness
In the early hours of the morning.[270]

FRIDAY PRAYER

LXII : 9

O ye who believe!
When the call is proclaimed
To prayer on Friday[271]
(The Day of Assembly),

269. *Sabr* (*Sabirin*) includes many shades of meaning: I have specified three here, *viz.*, Patience, firmness and self-control

270. They have faith. humility, and hope, and they have certain virtues *viz.*: (1) patience. steadfastness, self-restraint and all that goes under the full definition of Sabr; this shows a certain attitude of mind; (2) in all their dealings they are true and sincere as they are also in their promises and words; this marks them out in social conduct: (3) further. their spiritual worship is earnest and deep, an inner counterpart of their outward conduct; (4) their worship of God shows itself in their love of their fellow men, for they are ready and liberal in charity; and (5) their self-discipline is so great that the first thing they do every morning is humbly to approach their God.

271. Friday, "the Muslim Sabbath" is primarily the Day of Assembly, the weekly meeting of the Congregation when we show our unity by sharing in common public worship, preceded

Hasten earnestly to the Remembrance
Of God, and leave off
Business (and traffic):[272]
That is best for you
If ye but knew![273]

by a Khutba, in which the Imam (or Leader) reviews the week's spiritual life of the community and offers advice and exhortation on holy living. Notice the gradations of social contact for Muslims if they followed the wise ordinances of their Faith. (1) Each individual remembers God for himself or herself five or more times every day, in the home or place of business, or local mosque, or open air, as the case may be. (2) On Friday in every week, there is a local meeting in the central mosque of each local centre,—it may be a village, or town, or ward of a big city. (3) At the two Ids every year, there is a larger local area meeting in one centre, the id-gah. (4) Once at least in a lifetime, where possible, a Muslim shares in the vast international assemblage of the world, in the centre of Islam at the Meccan Pilgrimage, A happy combination of decentralization and centralization of individual liberty and collective meeting, and contact at various stages or grades. The mechanical part of this ordinance is easy to carry out. Are we carrying out the more difficult part?—The spirit of unity, brotherhood, mutual consultation, and collective understanding and action?

272. The idea behind the Muslim weekly "Day of Assembly" is different from that of behind the Jewish Sabbath (Saturday) or the Christian Sunday. The Jewish Sabbath is primarily a commemoration of God's ending His works and resting on the seventh day (Gen ii. 2; Exod xx. 11): we are taught that God needs no rest, nor does He feel fatigue. The Jewish command forbids work on that day but says nothing about worship or prayer (Exod. xx 10); our ordinance lays chief stress on the remembrance of God. Jewish formalism went so far as to kill the spirit of the sabbath, and call forth the protest of Jesus: "the sabbath was made for man, and not man for the sabbath" **(Mark ii. 27) But the Christian Church, although it has changed the day from Saturday to Sunday, has inherited the Jewish spirit: witness the Scottish Sabbath; except in so far as it has been secularized. Our teaching says: "when the time for Jumu'a Prayer comes, close your business and answer the summons loyally and earnestly, meet earnestly, pray, consult and learn by social contact: when the meeting is over, scatter and go about your business".**

273. The immediate and temporal worldly gain may be the ultimate and spiritual loss, and *vice versa*.

GLORIFY LORD

XXXIII : 41 and 42

41. O ye who believe !
Celebrate the praises of God,
And do this often ;
42. And glorify Him
Morning and evening.

MIDDLE PRAYER

II : 238 and 239

238. Guard strictly
Your (habit of) prayers,
Especially the Middle prayer ;[274]
And stand before God
In a devout (frame of mind).
239. If ye fear (an enemy),[275]
Pray on foot, or riding
(As may be most convenient),
But when ye are

274. *The Middle Prayer*: *Salatul wusta*: may be translated "the best or the most excellent prayer" Authorities differ as to the exact meaning of this phrase. The weight of authorities seems to be in favour of interpreting this as the Asr prayer (in the middle of the afternoon). This is apt to be most neglected, and yet this is the most necessary, to remind us of God in the midst of our worldly affairs. There is a special Sura (ciii) entitled Asr, of which the mystic meaning is appropriately dealt with under that Sura.

275 *Vv.* 238-39 are parenthetical, introducing the subject of prayer in danger.

In security, celebrate
God's praises in the manner
He has taught you,
Which ye knew not (before).

REGULAR PRAYER

XI : 114

And establish regular Prayers
At the two ends of the day[276]
And at the approaches of the night:[277]
For those things that are good
Remove those that are evil:[278]

276. *The two ends of the day*: Morning and afternoon. The morning prayer is the *Fajr*, after the light is up but before sunrise: we thus get up betimes and begin the day with the remembrance of God and of our duty to Him, just as an ambassador might start on his journey after saluting his king and receiving his blessing. The early afternoon prayer, *Zuhr*, is immediately afternoon: we are in the midst of our daily life, and again we remember God.

277. *Approaches of the night*: *Zulafun*, plural of *Zulfatun*, an approach, something near at hand. As Arabic has, like Greek, a dual number distinct from the plural, and the plural number is used here, and not the dual, it is reasonable to agrue late that at least three "approaches of the night" are meant. The late afternoon prayer, *Asr*, can be one of these three, and the evening prayer, *Magrib*, just after sunset, can be the second. The early night prayer, *Isha*, at supper time when the glow of sunset is disappearing, would be the third of the "approaches of the night", when we commit ourselves to God before sleep. These are the five canonical prayers of Islam.

278. "*Those things that are good*": in this context the words refer primarily to prayers and sacred thoughts, but they include all good thoughts, good words and good deeds. It is by them that we keep away everything that is evil, whether referring to the past, the present, or the future.

Be that the word of remembrance
To those who remember (their Lord).

XVII: 78

Establish regular prayers—[279]
At the sun's decline
Till the darkness of the night,
And the morning prayer
And reading: for the prayer
And reading in the morning
Carry their testimony [280]

NAMAZ RESTRAINS FROM SHAMEFUL ACTS

XXIX: 45

Recite what is sent [281]
Of the Book by inspiration

279. The Commentators understand here the Command for the five daily canoncal prayers, *viz.* : the four from the declination of the sun from the zenith to the fullest darkness of the night and the early morning prayer, Fajr, which is usually accompanied by a reading of the Holy Quran. The four afternoon prayers are Zuhr immediately after the sun begins to decline in the afternoon ; Asr in the late afternoon ; Magrib immediately after sunset, and Isha, after the glow of sunset has disappeared and the full darkness of the night has set in. There is difference of opinion as to the meaning of particular words and phrases but none as to the general effect of the passage.

280. The morning prayer is specially singled out for separate mention, because the morning is a " holy hour " and special spiritual influences act on the soul awaking from the night's rest. Special testimony is borne to the prayers of this hour by the angelic host.

281. The *tilawat* of the Quran implies : (1) rehearsing or reciting it, and publishing it abroad to the world ; (2) reading it to ourselves ; (3) studying it to understand it as it should be

To thee, and establish
Regular Prayer: for Prayer
Restrains from shameful
And unjust deeds;
And remembrance of God
Is the greatest (thing in life)
Without doubt. And God knows
The (plans) that ye form.

SEEK HELP FROM NAMAZ

II: 153

O ye who believe! Seek help
With patient Perseverance [282]
And Prayer: for God is with those
Who patiently persevere.

IN TRAVEL

IV: 101

When ye travel
Through the earth,

studied and understood; (4) meditating on it so as to accord our knowledge and life and desires with it. When this is done, it merges into real Prayer, and Prayer purges us of anything (act plan, thought, motive, words) of which we should be ashamed or which would work injustice to others. Such Prayer passes into our inmost life and being, for then we realise the Presence of God, and that is true *zikr* (or remembrance), for remembrance is the bringing to mind of things as present to us which might otherwise be absent to us. And that is the greatest thing in life. It is subjective to us: it fills our consciousness with God. For God is in any case always present and knows all.

282. An additional meaning implied in *Sabr* is self-restraint. Haqqani defines it in his *Tafsir* as following Reason and restraining Fear, Anger and Desire. What can be a higher reward for

There is no blame on you
If ye shorten your prayers,[283]
For fear the Unbelievers
May attack you:
For the Unbelievers are
Unto you open enemies.

patience, perseverance, self restraint and constancy than that God should be with us? For this promise opens the door to every kind of spiritual well-being.

283. Verse 101 gives permission to shorten congregational prayers when people are on a journey. Vv. 102 and 103 deal with cases when they are in danger at war, in face of the enemy. The shortening of congregational prayers in both cases is further governed as to details by the practice of the Apostle and his Companions. As to journeys, two questions arise: (1) what constitutes a journey for this purpose? (2) Is the fear of an attack as essential condition for the shortening of congregational prayers? As to (1), it is best to leave the matter to discretion, having regard to all the circumstances of the journey, as in the case of the journeys which excuse a fast. The text leaves it to discretion. As to (2), the practice of the Apostle shows that danger is not an essential condition: it is merely mentioned as a possible incident. The Apostle usually shortened the prayers from four Rakats to two Rakats in *Zuhr* (midday prayer), *Asr* (afternoon prayer) and *Ishaa* (night prayer): the other two are in any case short *Fajr* (morning prayer) having two Rakats and *Magrib* (evening prayer) having three.

IX.—PROPHETS

APOSTLES TO ALL PEOPLE

X : 47

To every people (was sent)
An Apostle : when their Apostle[284]
Comes (before them), the matter
Will be judged between them
With justice, and they
Will not be wronged.

APOSTLE'S DUTY

XXIV : 54

Say : "Obey God, and obey
His Apostle : but if ye turn
Away, he is only responsible
For the duty placed on him
And ye for that placed
On you. If ye obey him,

284. Every people or generation or nation had its Message or Messenger : God revealed Himself to it in some way or another. If that Massenger was ignored or rejected, or His Message was twisted or misused, the Day of Reckoning will come. when perfect justice will be done and the whole Truth revealed. The Unbelievers mockingly say : "If that is true, pray tell us when that Day will come !" The answer of the Messenger is : "It will come in good time : no one can either hasten or

Ye shall be on right guidance.
The Apostle's duty is only
To preach the clear (Message).[285]

GENTLE NATURE OF PROPHET

III : 159

It is part of the Mercy
Of God that thou dost deal
Gently with them.[286]
Wert thou severe
Or harsh-hearted,
They would have broken away
From thee : so pass over
(Their faults), and ask
For God's forgiveness
For them ; and consult

retard it. If you want me then to save you or if you fear that I shall harm you for your treatment of me, know that this matter is in the hands of God alone, Who will do perfect justice. Even in regard to myself, any harm or good that befalls me is by the command and in the power of God."

285. If you disobey God's commands as explained by His Apostle, you are not going to be forced. The Apostle's mission is to train your will and explain clearly all the implications of your conduct. The responsibility for your conduct rests entirely on yourselves.

286. The extremely gentle nature of Mohammad endeared him to all, and it is reckoned as one of the Mercies of God. One of the Apostle's titles is "A Mercy to all Creation" At no time was this gentleness, this mercy, this long-suffering with human weaknesses, more valuable than after a disaster like that at Uhud. It is a God-like quality, which then, as always, bound and binds the souls of countless men to him.

Them in affairs (of moment).
Then, when thou hast
Taken a decision,
Put thy trust in God.
For God loves those
Who put their trust (in Him).

INSPIRATION TO PROPHET

XXI : 25

Not an apostle did We
Send before thee without
This inspiration sent by Us
To him : that there is
No god but I ; therefore
Worship and serve Me.

NO DISTINCTION BETWEEN PROPHETS

II : 285

The Apostle believeth
In what hath been revealed
To him from his Lord,
As do the men of faith.
Each one (of them) believeth
In God, His angels,
His books and His Apostles.[287]
" We make no distinction (they say)

287. This Sura started with the question of Faith, showed us various aspects of Faith, and the denial of Faith, gave us ordinances for the new People of Islam as a community,

Between one and another[288]
Of his Apostles." And they say:
" We hear, and we obey:
(We seek) Thy forgiveness,[289]
Our Lord, and to Thee
Is the end of all journeys."

IV : 152

To those who believe
In God, and His Apostles
And make no distinction
Between any of the Apostles,
We shall soon give
Their (due) rewards:
For God is Oft-forgiving
Most Merciful.

III : 84

Say: " We believe
In God, and in what

and now rounds off the argument again with a confession of Faith and of its practical manifestation in conduct ("we hear and we obey "), and closes on a note of humility, so that we may confess our sins, ask for forgiveness, and pray for God's help and guidance.

288. It is not for *us* to make any distinction between one and another of God's Apostles: we must honour them all equally, though we know that God in His wisdom sent them with different kinds of mission and gave them different degrees of rank.

289. When our faith and conduct are sincere, we realise how far from perfection we are, and we humbly pray to God for the forgiveness of our sins. We feel that God imposes no burden on us that we cannot bear, and with this realisation in our hearts and in the confession of our lips, we go to Him and ask for His help and guidance.

Has been revealed to us
And to Abraham, Ismail,
Isaac, Jacob, and the Tribes,
And in (the Books)
Given to Moses, Jesus,
And the Prophets,
From their Lord:
We make no distinction
Between one and another
Among them, and to God
Do we submit (in Islam)."

II : 136

Say ye : " We believe
In God, and the revelation
Given to us, and to Abraham,
Ismail, Isaac, Jacob,
And the Tribes, and that given
To Moses and Jesus, and that given
To the other Apostles from their Lord:
We make no difference
Between one and another of them :
For we bow to God (in Islam).[290]

290. Here we have the Creed of Islam : to believe in (1) the One Universal God, (2) the Message to us through Muhammad and the Signs (*ayat*) as interpreted on the basis of personal responsibility ; (3) the Message delivered by other Teachers in the past. These are mentioned in three groups : (1) Abraham, Ismail, Isaac, Jacob, and the Tribes: of these Abraham had apparently a Book and the others followed his tradition ; (2) Moses and Jesus, who each left a scripture ; these scriptures are still extant, though not in their pristine form ; and (3) other scriptures, Apostles or Messengers of God, not specifically mentioned in the Quran. We make no difference between any of these. Their Message (in essentials) was one, and that is the basis of Islam.

PROPHET A PATTERN

XXXIII : 21

Ye have indeed
In the Apostle of God
A beautiful pattern (of conduct)
For any one whose hope is [291]
In God and the Final Day,
And who engages much
In the praise of God.

UNLETTERED

VII : 158 (end)

So believe
In God and His Apostle,
The unlettered Prophet,[292]
Who believeth in God
And His Words : follow him
That (so) ye may be guided.

291. We now have the psychology of the Believers.—God-fearing men, led by that pattern of men and of leaders, Muhammad Mustafa.

292. "Unlettered," as applied to the Prophet has three special significations : (1) He was not versed in human learning ; yet he was full of the highest wisdom, and had a most wonderful knowledge of the previous scriptures. This was a proof of his inspiration. It was a miracle of the highest kind, a "Sign", which every one could test then, and every one can test now. (2) All organized human knowledge tends to be crystallized, to acquire a partial bias or flavour of some "school" of thought. The highest Teacher had to be free from any such taint, just as a clean slate is necessary if a perfectly clear and bold message has to be written on it. (3) In iii : 20 the epithet is

WARNER

VII : 188

Say : " I have no power
Over any good or harm
To myself except as God
Willeth. If I had knowledge
Of the unseen, I should have
Multiplied all good, and no evil
Should have touched me :
I am but a warner,
And a bringer of glad tidings
To those who have faith ".[293]

---

applied to the Pagan Arabs, because, before the advent of Islam, they were unlearned. That the last and greatest of the Prophets should arise among them, and they and their language be made the vehicle of the new, full, and universal light, has also a meaning.

293. A warner to all, and a bringer of glad tidings to those who have faith because they will profit by the glad tidings. As every one is invited to Faith, the glad tidings are *offered* to all, but they are not necessarily accepted by all.

X.—PARENTS

KINDNESS TO PARENTS

XXXI : 14 and 15

14. And We have enjoined on man
(To be good) to his parents :
In travail upon travail
Did his mother bear him,
And in years twain [294]
Was his weaning : (hear
The command), " Show gratitude
To Me and to thy parents :
To Me is (thy final) Goal.
15. " But if they strive [295]
To make thee join
In worship with Me
Things of which thou hast

294. The set of milk teeth in a human child is completed at the age of two years, which is, therefore, the natural extreme limit for breast-feeding. In our artificial life the duration is much less.

295. Where the duty to man conflicts with the duty to God, it means that there is something wrong with the human will, and we should obey God rather than man. But even here, it does not mean that we should be arrogant or insolent To parents and those in authority, we must be kind, considerate, and courteous, even where they command things which we should not do and therefore disobedience becomes our highest duty.

The worship of things other than God is the worship of false things, things which are alien to our true knowledge, things that go against our own pure nature as created by God.

No knowledge, obey them not;
Yet bear them company
In this life with justice
(And consideration), and follow
The way of those who
Turn to Me (in love): [296]
In the End the return
Of you all is to Me,
And I will tell you
The truth (and meaning) [297]
Of all that ye did."

XXIX : 8

We have enjoined on man
Kindness to parents: but if
They (either of them) strive
(To force) thee to join
With Me (in worship)
Anything of which thou hast

296. In any apparent conflict of duties our standard should be God's Will, as declared to us by His command. That is the way of those who love God: and their motive in disobedience to parents or human authority where disobedience is necessary by God's Law, is not self-willed rebellion or defiance, but love of God, which means the true love of man in the highest sense of the word. And the reason we should give is: "Both you and I have to return to God; therefore not only must I follow God's Will, but you must command nothing against God's Will."

297. These conflicts may appear to us strange and puzzling in this life. But in God's Presence we shall see their real meaning and significance. It may be that that was one way in which our true mettle could be tested: for it is not easy to disobey and love man at the same time.

No knowledge,[298] obey them not.
Ye have (all) to return
To Me and I will
Tell you (the truth)
Of All that ye did.[299]

II : 83

And remember we took[300]
A Covenant from the Children
Of Israel (to this effect) :
Worship none but God ;
Treat with kindness
Your parents and kindred,
And orphans and those in need ;
Speak fair to the people ;
Be steadfast in prayer ;
And practise regular charity.

298. That is, no certainty, in virtue of the spiritual light. In matters of faith and worship, even parents have no right to force their children. They cannot and must not hold up before them any worship but that of the One True God.

299. Children and parents must all remember that they have all to go before God's tribunal, and answer each for his own deeds. In cases where one set of people have lawful authority over another set of people (as in the case of parents and children, and the two differ in important matters like that of Faith, the latter are justified in rejecting authority : the apparent conflict will be solved when the whole truth is revealed to all eyes in the final Judgment.

300. So far from the Covenant being of the kind you suggest the real Covenant is about the moral law, which is set out in v. 83. This moral law is universal, and if you break it, no privileges will lighten your punishment or help you in any way : "Speak fair to the people" not only means outward courteasy from the leaders to the meanest among the people, but the protection of the people from being exploited, deceived, defrauded, or doped with things to lull their intelligence.

Thon did yc turn back,
Except a few among you,
And ye backslide (even now).

XLVI : 15

We have enjoined on man [301]
Kindness to his parents:
In sorrow did his mother
Bear him, and in sorrow
Did she give him birth.
The carrying of the (child)
To his weaning is
(A period of) thirty months [302]
At length, when he reaches
The age of full strength [303]

301. *Cf.* xxix. 8 and xxxi. 14.

302. In xxxi. 14 the time of weaning was stated to be at the age of 2 years, *i.e.*, 24 months. That leaves six months as the *minimum* period of human gestation after which the child is known to be viable. This is in accordance with the latest ascertained scientific facts. The *average* period is 280 days, or ten times the intermenstrual period, and of course the average period of weaning is much less than 24 months.

The maximum period of breast-feeding (2 years) is again in accordance with the time that the first dentition is ordinarily completed in a human child. The lower milk incisors in the centre come out between the 6th and 9th month; then come out the milk teeth at intervals, until the canines appear. The second molars come out at about 24 months, and with them the child has a complete apparatus of milk teeth. Nature now expects him to chew and masticate and be independent of his mother's milk completely. On the other hand it hurts the mother to feed from the breast after the child has a complete set of milk teeth. The permanent teeth begin at the 6th year, and the second molars come at 12 years. The third molars are the wisdom teeth which may appear at 18 to 20 years, or not at all.

303. The age of full strength (*ashudd*) is held to be between 18 or 30 to 32. Between 30 and 40 thc man is in his best

And attains forty years,
He says, "O my Lord!
Grant me that I may be
Grateful for Thy favour
Which Thou hast bestowed
Upon me, and upon both
My parents, and that I
May work righteousness
Such as Thou mayest approve;
And be gracious to me
In my issue. Truly
Have I turned to Thee
And truly do I bow
To Thee in Islam."

XVII : 23 to 25

23. Thy Lord hath decreed
That ye worship none but Him,
And that ye be kind
To parents. Whether one
Or both of them attain
Old age in thy life,[304]
Say not to them a word
Of contempt, nor repel them,

manhood. After that he begins to look to his growing issue, and rightly commends the new generation to God. Perhaps his spiritual faculties also gain the upper hand after 40.

304. The spiritual and moral duties are now brought into juxtaposition. We are to worship none but God, because none but God is worthy of worship, not because "the Lord thy God is a jealous God, visiting the inequity of the fathers upon the children unto the third and fourth generation of them that hate Me" (Exod. xx : 5).

But address them
In terms of honour.
24. And, out of kindness,
Lower to them the wing[305]
Of humility, and say:
"My Lord! bestow on them
Thy Mercy even as they
Cherished me in childhood."[306]
25. Your Lord knoweth best
What is in your hearts:
If ye do deeds of righteousness,
Verily He is Most Forgiving
To those who turn to Him
Again and again (in true penitence).[307]

Note that the act of worship may be collective as well as individual, hence the plural *ta'budu*. The kindness to parents is an individual act of piety; hence the singular *Taqul, qul*, etc.

305. The metaphor is that of a high-flying bird which lowers her wing out of tenderness to her offspring. There is a double aptness: (1) when the parent was strong and the child was helpless, parental affection was showered on the child: when the child grows up and is strong, and the parent is helpless, can he do less than bestow similar tender care on the parent? (2) But more: he must approach the matter with gentle humility: for does not parental love remind him of the great love with which God cherishes his creatures? There is something here more than simple human gratitude: it goes up into the highest spiritual region

306. Note that we are asked to honour our father and mother, not "that thy days may be long upon the land which the Lord thy God giveth thee" (Exod. xx : 12), but upon much higher and more universal grounds, such as befit a perfected revelation. In the first place, not merely respect, but cherishing kindness, and humility to parents, are commanded. In the second place, this command is bracketted with the command to worship the One True God: parental love should be to us a type of divine love: nothing that we can do can ever really compensate for that which we have received. In the third place (see next verse) our spiritual advancement is tested by this: we cannot expect God's forgiveness if we are rude or unkind to those who unselfishly brought us up.

307. It is the heart, and its hidden and secret motives, by which we are judged: for God knows them all.

XI.—QURAN

CONFIRMS SCRIPTURES

V : 51 (part)

To thee We sent a Scripture
In truth, confirming
The scripture that came
Before it, and guarding it [308]
In safety: so judge
Between them by what
God hath revealed,
And follow not their vain
Desires, diverging
From the Truth that hath come
To thee.

GUIDE

XVI : 64

And We sent down the Book
To thee for the express purpose,

308. After the corruption of the older revelations, the Quran comes with a twofold purpose: (1) to confirm the true and original Message, and (2) to guard it, or act as a check to its interpretation. For example, if people seek retaliation in a spirit of revenge, it holds forth mercy. If they glibly mask their cowardice or sentimentalism by empty talk of "turning the other cheek," it tests them by the practical test of forgiveness and mercy.

That thou shouldst make clear
To them those things in which[309]
They differ, and that it should be
A guide and a mercy
To those who believe.

III : 138

Here is a plain statement
To men, a guidance
And instruction to those
Who fear God!

MEASURE

LXXIII : 4

And recite the Quran [309-A]
In slow, measured rhythmic tones.

309. But the path of duty before God's Messenger is clear. He is sent with the Revelation (the Quran) for three express purposes : (1) that he should bring about unity, among the jarring sects, for the Gospel of Unity, while preaching the One True God, leads also to the unity of mankind; (2) that the revelation should be a guide to right conduct; and (3) that it should show the path of repentance and salvation, and thus be the highest mercy to erring sinners.

309-A. At this time there was only xciv., lxvii. and possibly lxxiv. and the opening Sura (Al-Hamd): but the heart of the Apostle had received enlightenment, and that Light was gradually fading expression in the verses of the Quran. For us, now, with the whole of the Quran before us, the injunction is specially necessary. The words of the Quran must not be read hastily, merely to get through so much reading. They must be studied and their meaning pondered over. They are themselves so beautiful that they must be lovingly pronounced in tones of rhythmic music.

POWERFUL

LIX : 21

Had We sent down
This Quran on a mountain,[310]
Verily, thou wouldst have seen
It humble itself and cleave
Asunder for fear of God.
Such are the similitudes
Which We propound to men,
That they may reflect.

II : 121

Those to whom we have sent
The Book study it
As it should be studied :
They believe therein :
Those who reject faith therein,—
The loss is their own.

STUDY

XLVII : 24

Do they not then
Earnestly seek to understand
The Quran, to are
Their hearts locked up
By them ?

310. There are two ideas associated in men's minds with a mountain ; one is its height, and the other that it is rocky, stony, hard. Now comes the metaphor. The Revelation of God is so sublime, that even the highest mountains humble themselves before it. The Revelation is so powerful and convincing that even the hard rock splits asunder under it. Will man then be so arrogant as to consider himself superior to it, or so hard-hearted as not to be affected by its powerful Message ? The answer is "No" for unspoilt man ; "Yes" for man when degraded by sin to be the vilest of creatures.

VERSES BASIC

XI : 1 to 3

1. (This is) a Book,
With Verses basic or fundamental [311]
(Of established meaning)
Further explained in detail,—
From One Who is Wise
And Well-acquainted (with all things) :
2. (It teacheth) that ye should
Worship none but God
(Say :) " Verily I am [312]
(Sent) unto you from Him
To warn and to bring
Glad tidings :
3. " (And to preach thus), ' Seek ye
The forgiveness of your Lord,
And turn to Him in repentance ;
That He may grant you
Enjoyment, good (and true),
For a term appointed,
And bestow His abounding grace
On all who abound in merit ! [313]
But if ye turn away,
Then I fear for you
The Penalty of a Great Day :

311. Every basic principle is included in God's Revelation, and it is further illustrated and explained in detail.

312. Mustafa's Message—as was the Message of all Apostles—was to warn against evil, and to bring the glad tidings of God's Mercy and Grace to all who would receive it in Faith and trust in God. This double Message is preached illustratively in this Sura.

313. The enjoyment of all good and true things in life refers, I think, to the present life with its limited term, and the abounding Grace refers to the higher spiritual reward, which begins here but is completed in the life to come.

XII.—WOMEN AND WIVES

REHEARSE GOD'S FAVOUR

II : 231 part

Do not treat God's Signs
As a jest[314]
But solemnly rehearse[315]
God's favours on you,
And the fact that He
Sent down to you
The Book
And Wisdom,
For your instruction.
And fear God,
And know that God
Is well acquainted
With all things.

314. These difficult questions of sex relations are often treated as a joke. But they profoundly affect out individual lives, the lives of our children, and the purity and well-being of the society in which we live. This aspect of the question is reiterated again and again.

315. We are asked to remember in our own minds, and to proclaim and praise, and be proud, of God's favours on us. His favours are immeasurable : not the least are His Revelations, and the wisdom which He has given to us to enable us to judge and act up to His guidance.

DIVORCE PERMISSIBLE

II : 230 (part)

So if a husband
Divorces his wife (irrevocably),[316]
He cannot, after that,
Re-marry her until
After she has married
Another husband and
He has divorced her.
In that case there is
No blame on either of them
If they re-unite, provided
They feel that they
Can keep the limits
Ordained by God.

II : 236 and 237 (part)

236. There is no blame on you
If ye divorce women
Before consummation
Or the fixation of their dower;
But bestow on them
(A suitable gift),
The wealthy
According to his means,

316. Two divorces followed by re-union are permissible; the third time the divorce becomes irrevocable, until the woman marries some other man and he divorces her. This is to set an almost impossible condition. The lesson is : if a man loves a woman he should not allow a sudden gust of temper or anger to induce him to take hasty action. What happens after two divorces, if the man takes her back ? See *v.* 231.

And the poor
According to his means ;—
A gift of a reasonable amount
Is due from those
Who wish to do the right thing.
237. And if ye divorce them
Before consummation,
But after the fixation
Of a dower for them,
Then the half of the dower
(Is due to them), unless
They remit it
Or (the man's half) is remitted [317]
By him in whose hands
Is the marriage tie ;[318]

II : 228

Divorced women
Shall wait concerning themselves
For three monthly periods.
Nor it is lawful for them
To hide what God
Hath created in their wombs,
If they have faith
In God and the Last Day.

317. The law declares that in such a case half the dower fixed shall be paid by the man to the woman. But it is open to the woman to remit the half due to her or to the man to remit the half which he is entitled to deduct, and thus pay the whole.

318. *Him in whose hands is the marriage tie* : According to Hanafi doctrine this is the husband himself, who can ordinarily by his act dissolve the marriage. It therefore behoves him to be all the more liberal to the woman and pay her the full dower even if the marriage was not consummated.

And their husbands
Have the better right
To take them back
In that period, if
They wish for reconciliation.[319]
And women shall have rights
Similar to the rights
Against them, according
To what is equitable ;
But men have a degree
(Of advantage) over them.[320]
And God is Exalted, Wise.

II : 241

For divorced women
Maintenance (should be provided)
On a reasonable (scale).

319. Islam tries to maintain the married state as far as possible especially where children are concerned, but it is against the restriction of the liberty of men and women in such vitally important matters as love and family life. It will check hasty action as far as possible, and leave the door to reconciliation open at many stages. Even after divorce a suggestion of reconciliation is made, subject to certain precautions against thoughtless action. A period of waiting (*iddat*) for three monthly courses is prescribed, in order to see if the marriage conditionally dissolved is likely to result in issue. But this is not necessary where the divorced woman is a virgin: It is definitely declared that women and men shall have similar rights against each other.

320. The difference in economic position between the sexes makes the man's rights and liabilities a little greater than the woman's. The duty of the man is to maintain the woman, and so a certain difference in nature between the sexes. Subject to this, the sexes are on terms of equality in law, and in certain matters the weaker sex is entitled to special protection.

This is a duty
On the righteous.

IV : 4

And give the women
(On marriage) their dower,
As a free gift ; but if they,
Of their own good pleasure,
Remit any part of it to you,
Take it and enjoy it
With right good cheer.

FAMILY DISPUTES, RULES REGARDING

IV : 128

If a wife fears
Cruelty or desertion
On her husband's part,
There is no blame on them
If they arrange
An amicable settlement
Between themselves ;
And such settlement is best ;
Even though men's souls
Are swayed by greed.[321]

321. To protect the woman's economic interests, various rules are prescribed for dower in marriage. But the sanctity of marriage itself is greater than any economic interests Divorce is, of all things permitted, most hateful to God. Therefore if a breach between husband and wife can be prevented by some economic consideration, it is better to make that concession than to imperil the future of the wife, the children, and probably the husband also. Such concessions are permissible, in view of

But if ye do good
And practise self-restraint,
God is well-acquainted
With all that ye do.

IV : 34 and 35

34. Men are the protectors
And maintainers of women,
Because God has given
The one more (strength)
Than the other, and because
They support them
From their means.
Therefore the righteous women
Are obedient, and guard
In (the husband's) absence
What God would have them guard.[322]
As to those women
On whose part ye fear
Disloyalty and ill-conduct,

the love of wealth ingrained in unregenerate man, but a recommendation is made that we should practise self-restraint, and do what we can to come to an amicable settlement without any economic sacrifice on the part of the woman.

322. Or the sentence may be rendered : "and protect (the husband's interests) in his absence, as God has protected them." If we take the rendering as in the text, the meaning is : the good wife is obedient and harmonious in her husband's presence, and in his absence guards his reputation and property and her own virtue, as ordained by God. If we take the rendering as in the note, we reach the same result in a different way, the good wife : in her husband's absence, remembering how God has given her a sheltered position, does everything to justify that position by guarding her own virtue and his reputation and property.

Admonish them (first),[323]
(Next), refuse to share their beds,
(And last) beat them lightly;
But if they return to obedience,
Seek not against them[324]
Means (of annoyance):
For God is Most High,
Great (above you all).

35. If ye fear a breach
Between them twain,
Appoint two arbiters,
One from his family,
And the other from hers;[325]
If they wish for peace,
God will cause
Their reconciliation:
For God hath full knowledge,
And is acquainted

323. In case of family jars four steps are mentioned, to be taken in that order: (1) perhaps verbal advice or admonition may be sufficient; (2) if not, sex relations may be suspended; (3) if this is not sufficient, some slight physical correction may be administered; but Imam Shafi considers this inadvisable, though permissible, and all authorities are unanimous in deprecating any sort of cruelty, even of the nagging kind, as mentioned in the next clause; (4) if all this fails, a family counsel is recommended in *v.* 35 below.

324. Temper, nagging, sarcasm, speaking at each other in other people's presence, reverting to past faults which should be forgiven and forgotten,—all this is forbidden. And the reason given is characteristic of Islam. You must live all your life as in the presence of God, Who is high above us, but Who watches over us. How petty and contemptible will our little squabbles appear in His presence!

325. An excellent plan for settling family disputes, without too much publicity or mud-throwing, or resort to the chicaneries of the law. The Latin countries recognize this plan in their legal systems. It is a pity that Muslims do not resort to it universally, as they should. The arbiters from each family would know the idiosyncracies of both parties, and would be able, with God's help, to effect a real reconciliation.

With all things.

IV : 19 (part)

On the contrary live with them
On a footing of kindness and equity.
If ye take a dislike to them,
If may be that ye dislike
A thing, and God brings about
Through it a great deal of good.

GUILTY OF LEWDNESS

IV : 15 and 16

15. If any of your women
Are guilty of lewdness,[326]
Take the evidence of four[327]
(Reliable) witnesses from amongst you
Against them; and if they testify,
Confine them to houses until
Death do claim them
Or God ordain for them,

326. Most commentators understand this to refer to adultery or fornication; in that case they consider that the punishment was altered to 100 stripes. But I think it refers to unnatural crime between women, analogous to unnatural crime between men in *v.* 16 below; because (1) no punishment is specified here for the man, as would be the case where a man was involved in the crime; (2) the word *Al-lāti*, the purely feminine plural of *Al-lati* is used for the parties to the crime; (3) the punishment is indefinite, see the next note but one.

327. To protect the honour of women, stricter evidence is required, *i.e.*, the evidence of four instead of the usual two witnesses. It is the same for adultery.

Some (other) way[328]
16. If two men among you
Are guilty of lewdness,
Punish them both.
If they repent and amend,
Leave them alone ; for God
Is Oft-returning, Most Merciful.

IV : 3

If ye fear that ye shall not
Be able to deal justly
With the orphans,[329]
Marry women of your choice
Two, or three, or four ;
But if ye fear that ye shall not

328. Keep them in their houses until some definite order s received. Those who take the crime to be adultery or fornication construe this definite order ("some other way") to mean some definite pronouncement by the Prophet under inspiration ; this was the punishment of flogging. If we understand the crime to be unnatural crime, we might presume, in the absence of any definite order ("some other way") that the punishment would be similar to that for men in the next verse. That is itself indefinite, and perhaps intentionally so, as the crime is most shameful, and should be unknown in a well-regulated society. The maximum punishment would of course be imprisonment for life.

329. Notice the conditional clause about orphans, introducing the rules about marriage. This reminds us of the immediate occasion of the promulgation of this verse. It was after Uhud, when the Muslim community was left with many orphans and widows, and some captives of war. Their treatment was to be governed by principles of the greatest humanity and equity. The occasion is past, but the principles remain. Marry the orphans if you are quite sure that you will in that way protect their interests and their property, with perfect justice to them and to your own dependants if you have any. If not, make other arrangements for the orphans.

be able to deal justly (with them),
Then only one, or (a captive)
That your right hands possess.
That will be more suitable,
To prevent you
From doing injustice.[330]

MORE THAN ONE ONLY IF YOU CAN BE PERFECTLY FAIR AND JUST TO ALL

IV : 129 and 130

129. Ye are never able
To be fair and just
As between women,
Even if it is
Your ardent desire :
But turn not away
(From a woman) altogether,
So as to leave her (as it were)
Hanging (in the air).[331]
If ye come to a friendly
Understanding, and practise

330. The unrestricted number of wives of the "Times of ignorance" was now strictly limited to a maximum of four, provided you could treat them with perfect equality, in material things as well as in affection and immaterial things. As this condition is most difficult to fulfil. I understand the recommendation to be towards monogamy.

331. In this material world there are two principal causes of division between man and wife, money and "the other woman" or "the other man." Money was dealt with in the last verse. Here is the case of "the the other woman." Legally more than one wife (up to four) are permissible on the condition

Self-restraint, God is
Oft-forgiving, Most Merciful.
130. But if they disagree
(And must part), God
Will provide abundance
For all from His
All-reaching bounty :
For God is He
That careth for all
And is Wise.

PROHIBITED

IV : 23 and 24

23. Prohibited to you
(For marriage) are :—[332]
Your mothers, daughters,[333]
Sisters ; Father's sisters,

hat the man can be perfectly fair and just to all. But this s a condition almost impossible to fulfil. If, in the hope that e might be able to fulfil it, a man puts himself in that impossible osition, it is only right to insist that he should not discard ne but at least fulfil all the outward duties that are incumbent n him in respect of her.

332. This Table of Prohibited Degrees agrees in the main vith what is usually accepted among all nations, except in ninor details. It begins in the last verse (with father's wives). The scheme is drawn up on the assumption that the person vho proposes to marry is a man : if it is a woman, the same cheme will apply, *mutatis mutandis* : it will read : "your fathers, ons, brothers," etc. ; or you can always read it from the usband's view of relationship, as there must always be a usband in a marriage.

333. "Mother" includes grandmother (through the father or nother), great-grand-mother, etc. ; "daughter" includes grand-laughter (through son or daughter), great-grand-daughter, etc. ; 'sister" includes full-sister and half-sister. "Father's sister" ncludes grandfather's sister, etc., and "mother's sister" includes grandmother's sister, etc.

Mother's sisters, Brother's daughters,
Sister's daughters, Foster-mothers [334]
(Who gave you suck), foster-sisters,
Your wives' mothers;
Your step-daughters under your [335]
Guardianship, born of your wives,
To whom ye have gone in,—
No prohibition if ye have not gone in;—
Wives of your sons [336] proceeding
from your loins
And two sisters in wedlock
At one and the same time,[337]
Except for what is past,
For God is Oft-forgiving
Most Merciful;—
24. Also (prohibited are)
Women already married,
Except those
Whom your right hands possess: [338]

334. "Fosterage" or milk relationships play an important part in Muslim Law and count like blood-relationships: it would therefore seem that not only foster-mothers and foster-sisters, but foster-mother's sister, etc., all come within the prohibited degrees.

335. It is generally (but not unanimously) held that "under your guardianship" is a description, not a condition. Therefore a step-daughter not "under your guardianship" is still within the prohibition if the other condition (about her mother) is fulfilled.

336. 'Sons' includes grandsons, but excludes adopted sons or persons treated as such, on account of the words "proceeding from your loins."

337. The bar against two sisters in marriage together applies o aunt and niece together, but not to deceased wife's sister after the wife dies.

338. *Whom your : right hands possess*: *i.e.*, captives in a Jihad,

Thus hath God ordained
(Prohibitions) gainst you :
Except for these, all others
Are lawful, provided
Ye seek (them in marriage)
With gifts from your property,—
Desiring chastity, not lust.[339]
Seeing that ye derive
Benefit from them, give them
Their dowers (at least)[340]
As prescribed ; but if,
After a dower is prescribed, ye agree
Mutually (to vary it)
There is no blame on you.
And God is All-knowing,
All-wise.

II : 221

Do not marry
Unbelieving women,

or war under orders of the righteous Imam against those who persecute Faith. In such cases formal hostility dissolves civil ties.

339. After defining the prohibited degrees, the verse proceeds to say that women other than those specified may be sought in marriage, but even so, not from motives of lust, but in order to promote chastity between the sexes. Marriage in the original Arabic is here described by a word which suggests a fortress (*hisn*) : marriage is, therefore, the fortress of chastity.

340. As the woman in marriage surrenders her person, so the man also must surrender (besides some part of his independence) at least some of his property according to his means. And this gives rise to the law of Dower. A minimum dower is prescribed, but it is not necessary to stick to the minimum, and in the new relationship created, the parties are recommended to act towards each other with the greatest confidence and liberality.

Until they believe:
A slave woman who believes
Is better than an unbelieving woman,
Even though she allure you.
Nor marry (your girls)
To unbelievers until
They believe:
A man slave who believes
Is better than an unbeliever,
Even though he allure you.[341]
Unbelievers do but
Beckon you to the Fire.
But God beckons by His Grace
To the Garden (of Bliss)
And forgiveness,
And makes His Signs
Clear to mankind:
That they may
Celebrate His praise.

MODESTY (PURDAH)

XXXIII : 59

O Prophet! Tell
Thy wives and daughters,

341. Marriage is a most intimate communion, and the mystery of sex finds its highest fulfilment when intimate spiritual harmony is combined with the physical link. If religion is at all the real influence in life to both parties, or to either party a difference in this vital matter must affect the lives of both more profoundly than differences of birth, race, language, or position in life. It is therefore only right that the parties to be married should have the same spiritual outlook. If two persons love each other, their outlook in the highest things of life must be the same. Note that religion is not here a mere label, or a matter of custom or birth. The two persons may have been born in different religions, but if, by their mutual influence, they come to see the truth in the same way, they must openly accept the same rites and the same social brotherhood. Otherwise the position will become impossible individually and socially.

And the believing women,[342]
That they should cast
Their outer garments over[343]
Their persons (when abroad),
That is most convenient,
That they should be known[344]
(As such) and not molested.
And God is Oft-forgiving,[345]
Most Merciful.

XXIV : 30 and 31

30. Say to the believing men
That they should lower
Their gaze and guard[346]
Their modesty : that will make

342. This is for all Muslim women, those of the Prophet's household, as well as the others. The times were those of insecurity and they were asked to cover themselves with outer garments when walking abroad. It was never contemplated that they should be confined to their houses like prisoners.

343. *Jilbab*, plural *jalabib* : an outer garment ; a long gown covering the whole body, or a cloak covering the neck and bosom.

344. The object was not to restrict the liberty of women, but to protect them from harm and molestation under the conditions then existing in Medina. In the East and in the West a distinctive public dress of some sort or another has always been a badge of honour or distinction, both among men and women. This can be traced back to the earliest civilzations. Asyrian Law in its palmiest days (say) 7th Century B.C. enjoined the veiling of married women and forbade the veiling of slaves and women of ill fame ; See Cambridge Ancient History III. 107.

345. This rule was not absolute : if for any reason it could not be observed, "God is Oft-returning, Most Merciful."

346. The rule of modesty applies to men as well as women.

For greater purity for them :
For God is well acquainted
With all that they do.
31. And say to the believing women
That they should lower
Their gaze and guard[347]
Their modesty ; that they
Should not display their
Beauty and ornaments[348] except
What (must ordinarily) appear
Thereof, that they should
Draw their veils over
Their bosoms and not display
Their beauty except
To their husbands, their fathers,
Their husbands' fathers, their sons,
Their husbands' sons,

A brazen stare by a man at a woman (or even at a man) is a breach of refined manners. Where sex is concerned, modesty is not only "good form": it is not only to guard the weaker sex, but also to guard the spiritual good of the stronger sex.

347. The need for modesty is the same in both men and women. But on account of the differentiation of the sexes in nature, temperaments, and social life, a greater amount of privacy is required for women than for men, especially in the matter of dress and the uncovering of the bosom.

348. *Zinat* means both natural beauty and artificial ornaments. I think both are implied here, but chiefly the former. The woman is asked not to make a display of her figure or appear in undress except to the following classes of people : (1) her husband ; (2) her near relatives who would be living in the same house, and with whom a certain amount of *neglige* is permissible; (3) her women, *i.e.*, her maid servants, who would be constantly in attendance on her ; Some commentators include all believing women ; it is not good form in a Muslim household for women to meet other women, except when they are properly dressed ; (4) Slaves, male and female, as they would be in constant attendance ; but this item would now be blank, with the abolition of slavery ; (5) old or infirm men-servants ; and (6) infants or small children before they get a sense of sex. *Cf.* also XXXIII. 59.

Their brothers or their brothers' sons,
Or their sisters' sons,
Or their women, or the slaves
Whom their right hands
Possess, or male servants
Free of physical needs,
Or small children who
Have no sense of the shame
Of sex; and that they
Should not strike their feet
In order to draw attention
To their hidden ornaments.[349]
And O ye Believers!
Turn ye all together
Towards God, that ye
May attain Bliss.[350]

SHARE IN INHERITANCE

IV: 7 and 8

7. From what is left by parents
And those nearest related[351]

349. It is one of the tricks of showy or unchaste women to tinkle their ankle ornaments, to draw attention to themselves.

350. While all these details of the purity and good form of domestic life are being brought to our attention, we are clearly reminded that the chief object we should hold in view is our spiritual welfare. All our brief life on this earth is a probation, and we must make our individual, domestic, and social life all contribute to our holiness, so that we can get the real success and bliss which is the aim of our spiritual endeavour. Mystics understand the rules of decorum themselves to typify spiritual truths. Our soul, like a modest maiden, allows not her eyes to stray from the One True God. And her beauty is not for vulgar show, but for God.

351. I have resisted the temptation to translate "next of

There is a share for men
And a share for women,
Whether the property be small
Or large, a determinate share.
8. But if at the time of division
Other relatives, or orphans
Or poor, are present,
Give them something also,
And speak to them
Words of kindness and justice.

II : 240

Those of you
Who die and leave widows
Should bequeath
For their widows
A year's maintenance
And residence ;[352]
But if they leave
(The residence),
There is no blame on you
For what they do

kin," as this phrase has a technical meaning in Indian Law, referring to certain kinds of heirs, whereas here the people meant are those whose inheritance is to be divided. The shares are specified. Here the general principles are laid down that females inherit as well as males, and that relatives who have no legal shares, orphans, and indigent people are not to be treated harshly, if present at the division.

352. Opinions differ whether the provision (of a year's maintenance, with residence), for a widow is abrogated by the share which the widow gets (one-eighth or one-fourth) as an heir. I do not think it is. The bequest (where made) takes effect as a charge on the property, but the widow can leave the house before the year is out, and presumably the maintenance then ceases.

With themselves,
Provided it is reasonable,
And God is Exalted, Wise.

WIDOWS

XXIV: 32

Marry those among you
Who are single,[353] or
The virtuous ones among
Your slaves, male or female:
If they are in poverty,
God will give them
Means out of his grace:
For God's bounty is for all,[354]
And He knows all things.

---

353. The subject of sex ethics and manners brings us to the subject of marriage. "Single" (*Ayama*, plural of *Aiyim*) here means any one not in the bond of wedlock, whether unmarried or lawfully divorced, or widowed. If we can, we must marry in our own circle, but if we have not the means, there is no harm if we choose from a lower circle, provided our choise is determined by virtue. Poverty in the other party does not matter if there is virtue and love. A happily married man has the best wealth in a virtuous wife, and his very happiness makes him a better potential earner of wealth. A slave becomes free by marriage.

354. God's mercy is for all: it is not confined to a class or grade of people.

A SELECTED BIBLIOGRAPHY

1. **Maulana Abul Kalam Azad** : *Tarjumanul Quran*, Arabic Text of Quran with Urdu translation, 2 Volumes. Price Rs. 7-8 per volume.—Sh. Muhammad Ashraf, Kashmiri Bazar, Lahore.

2. **Allama Abdullah Yusuf Ali** : Arabic Text of Quran and English Translation. Price Rs. 30.—Sh. Muhammad Ashraf, Kashmiri Bazar, Lahore.

3. **Maulana Shibli and Syed Suleiman Nadvi** : *Sirut-un-Nabi*. Five Volumes.—Dar-ul-Mosannifin, Azamgarh. Vol. I, Rs. 4 ; Vol. II, Rs. 3-8 ; Vol. III, Rs. 5 ; Vol. IV, Rs. 5-8 ; Vol. V, Rs. 4.

4. **Taj Company, Lahore** : Arabic Text with Urdu translation Rs. 15.

5. Quran by Anjuman Himayat Islam, Lahore. Price (according to quality of paper). Rs. 25 ; 5 and 3.

This edition is very nicely printed and free from errors, children read it with ease. Rs 3 edition is specially suitable for children, cheaper editions generally contain many mistakes and should not be placed in the hands of children. Anjuman Himayat Islam have rendered great service to Islam in bringing out this edition.

6. *The Great Prophet* and *Mohammad the Prophet*, by F. K. Khan Durrani, Editor, *The Truth*, Lahore.

7. *Lectures on Quran*—Syed Rashid Raza Misri, Seerat Committee Patti, District Lahore. Price Re. 1.

8. Allama Enayat Ullah Khan, Almashraki, *Qual-i-Faisal*, As. 2 ; *Tazkirah*, Rs. 5, Ichchra, Lahore.

9. *Musaddas Hali*—Hali Publishing House, Delhi.